OUR
DAILY
BREAD

D1413971

ALSO BY RALPH WRIGHT, OSB
PUBLISHED BY PAULIST PRESS

Christ—Our Love for All Seasons:
A Liturgy of the Hours for Everyone

OUR
DAILY
BREAD

GLIMPSING THE EUCHARIST
THROUGH THE CENTURIES

RALPH WRIGHT, OSB

Paulist Press
New York/Mahwah, NJ

Cover art: *The Last Supper* by Leonardo da Vinci.

Cover design by Joy Taylor
Book design by Lynn Else

Copyright © 2008 by Ralph Wright, OSB

All rights reserved. No part of this book may be reproduced or transmitted in any form or by any means, electronic or mechanical, including photocopying, recording, or by any information storage and retrieval system without permission in writing from the Publisher.

Library of Congress Cataloging-in-Publication Data

Wright, Ralph, OSB.
    Our daily bread : glimpsing the Eucharist through the centuries / Ralph Wright.
      p. cm.
    Includes bibliographical references and index.
    ISBN 978-0-8091-4525-6 (alk. paper)
    1. Lord's Supper—Catholic Church. 2. Lord's Supper Biblical teaching. 3. Lord's Supper—History. I. Title.
    BX2215.3.W75 2008
    234'.16309—dc22

                                  2007048007

Published by Paulist Press
997 Macarthur Boulevard
Mahwah, New Jersey 07430

www.paulistpress.com

Printed and bound in the
United States of America

For Laurence Kriegshauser, OSB

il miglior teologo

"Abide in me, and I in you" (John 15:4)

19. When the disciples on the way to Emmaus asked Jesus to stay "with" them, he responded by giving them a much greater gift: through the Sacrament of the Eucharist he found a way to stay "in" them. Receiving the Eucharist means entering into a profound communion with Jesus. "Abide in me, and I in you" (*Jn* 15:4). This relationship of profound and mutual "abiding" *enables us to have a certain foretaste of heaven on earth.* Is this not the greatest of human yearnings? Is this not what God had in mind when he brought about in history his plan of salvation? God has placed in human hearts a "hunger" for his word (cf. *Am* 8:11), a hunger which will be satisfied only by full union with him. Eucharistic communion was given so that we might be "sated" with God here on earth, in expectation of our complete fulfillment in heaven.

John Paul II, Mane Nobiscum

CONTENTS

CONTENTS

CONTENTS

CONTENTS

FOREWORD

As people mature, they find themselves caught up in experiences that take them out of the narrow bed of their own self-centeredness. For example, they lose themselves in the excitement of a crowd cheering their sports team on to victory. They are taken over by the lush sound of a symphonic orchestra, inviting them into a world they could never have created that carries them across centuries into a vast musical sea. They give themselves in love to another person, who becomes more important to them than they are to themselves. New worlds open up: the world of fans united in the excitement of a winning team, the world of aesthetic pleasure bringing together mind and soul, the world of hearts and lives united in the mutual self-sacrifice of genuine love.

Sometimes people hesitate before those worlds, afraid of losing themselves in giving themselves to something greater. On the banks of the Zambezi River in central Africa years ago, four men came out of the bush to inquire about meeting the local parish priest. Three went in to talk to the missionary; one stayed by the riverbank. When asked why he didn't join his friends, he explained that he knew what the priest was going to tell them: that God is all-loving and wants us to be happy in this life and the next, that God sent his Son to be our savior and that Jesus had left us ceremonies that made him present in our lives. He had heard it and had rejected it because he could not move beyond his own experience of hunger and disease, of misery and fear in his village. The story, the Gospel, was, he said, "too good to be true."

Hearing about the Holy Eucharist and attending the celebration of Mass bring a similar invitation to us. Our experience has to be opened, widened, and taken over by a world with Jesus Christ at the center. The awe and wonder thus glimpsed—greater than the possibility of being part of a winning team's experience, more pleasurable than a sea of sound, more self-involving than romantic love—can seem too beautiful to be real. Through the ages, all of us can and have drawn back from infinite love made concrete under the forms of bread and wine. We are afraid to love, to give ourselves, in a phrase of St. Augustine, to a "beauty ever ancient and ever new."

The Eucharist, which is the sign of the Church's unity in faith, has also been a source of profound disagreement among Christians since the Last Supper and Christ's sacrificial death on Calvary. The theological differences have also, however, occasioned a more profound understanding and greater appreciation of the vision that the apostolic faith presents. The Church's understanding grows as each generation of disciples experiences the self-sacrifice of Jesus Christ in the Eucharist. The Church's appreciation of this great gift increases as the courage to love is found in the experience of being loved by her Eucharistic Lord. Wherever the Eucharist is celebrated becomes the center of the universe, bringing all of us beyond the limitations of our own space and time, returning us then to a world made holier and more unified.

Fr. Ralph Wright is a Benedictine monk, one whose days are marked and unified by the rhythm of the Church's liturgical year. In this book he assembles the reflections and experiences of a "cloud of witnesses" (Heb 12:1), who accompany us through the ages in our following of Jesus Christ. Gathered together around the eucharistic banquet, we do "not grow weary or fainthearted" (Heb 12:3). To the words of these evangelists and martyrs, saints and theologians, Fr. Wright adds his own poetry, chapter by chapter, as a kind of Greek chorus, accompanying the unfolding of the mystery of faith over the years. As our lives surrender in awe to the wonder of the Eucharist, let our hearts fill with gratitude to God and also to the monk who puts together in this volume an invitation to enter more fully into the beauty that shapes the universe.

Francis Cardinal George, OMI
Archbishop of Chicago

PREFACE

This book is the indirect result of Pope John Paul II's encyclical on the Eucharist—*Ecclesia de Eucharistia* (2003). That work opened new doors for me onto this mystery, and I eventually decided to gather together a century-by-century glimpse of some aspect of the Eucharist, each viewed through the eyes of saints and classic writers. At the beginning of each century I've placed one of my own poems or hymns, whether an original or a translation, which is either directly or indirectly associated with this great *mysterium fidei*.

We start with St. Paul's Letter to the Corinthians, the earliest account of the Eucharist that has survived in writing; following that, to St. Mark—the earliest Gospel account of the institution; and then to chapter 6 of St. John's Gospel—the evangelist's account, perhaps forty or fifty years later, of Jesus as the Bread of Life. In Ignatius of Antioch, we catch the excitement of somebody moving toward Rome and the Coliseum with eucharistic imagery being the lens through which he describes his imminent martyrdom. Through Justin, we catch a "video-type presentation" of an early Sunday liturgy for a Christian assembly. In Cyprian, we find already expressed the apprehension that, through our serious sins, we might be separated from Christ's body and not be able to live that union with him which is salvation.

In the fourth and fifth centuries, we see the beginning of wondering *how* it all happens. *How* can it *be* the Body and Blood of Christ when it still looks like bread and wine? We find that early explanations insisted on the change that takes place at the consecration, and also that it is the Holy Spirit who effects this change. We need probe no further: after all it was the same Holy Spirit who effected the incarnation in Mary. All this time we find the emphasis that the Eucharist is to be, as St. Ambrose puts it, the daily medicine for the wound of our sinfulness, which is a daily phenomenon.

From St. Bede in the seventh century, we find that it is through this consecrated bread that we can live the life of God—"abide in me and I in you"—a life that we do not have access to, "unless you eat..." Moving on through time, we hear St. Symeon the New Theologian tell us how, through baptism and the Eucharist, we are restored to holiness, sinlessness, and freedom: we are no longer slaves to sin. Francis of Assisi reminds his priests to give themselves *totally* to God who, in an amazing way, comes through *their* hands to be upon the altar. Thomas Aquinas reminds us that the Incarnation is God's way of sharing his divinity with us; that nothing could be more wonderful than the Blessed Sacrament, through which we are given a foretaste of heaven; and that the apostles are given this gift of his presence to console them for his departure at the ascension.

In the late Middle Ages, Gertrude, Julian of Norwich, and Catherine of Siena all remind us of the personal love that Christ has for each of us and how this genuine love goes out of its way to disregard, as a Lover does, our shortcomings; Julian also illustrates how Jesus seeks to nurture us, like a mother feeding her child. Thomas à Kempis keeps the same theme—if you want to be with me, then I really want to be with you—the strong notion that God *wants* union with us as long as, through our own personal freedom (he always refuses to manipulate us), we genuinely want union with him. This theme is taken up centuries later by St. Alphonsus of Liguori.

In the last three centuries, the theme of uniting ourselves with Jesus' one sacrifice on Calvary is once more brought into prominence by Bl. Columba Marmion. The radiant presence of the Lord is adored by St. Philippine Duchesne on Holy Thursday night; and the joys of eucharistic adoration are described by Bl. Charles de Foucauld and Bl. Teresa of Calcutta.

The series of quotes comes to a conclusion with the temperate reflections of Pope Pius XII in his encyclical *Mediator Dei*. This reminds us that it is through the sacraments, and especially the Eucharist, that we personally affirm our desire to be incorporated into the Body of Christ in the union with God that Christ's redeeming death on Calvary has won for all people. Vatican II's call for the reform and renewal of the liturgy reminds us that the Mass is the source and summit of the Church's holiness. This brings us to John Paul's encyclical with which this book started. Finally, passages from Pope Benedict's postsynodal exhortation highlight the continuity that exists between his thought and that of his immediate predecessor.

The hymn "Highpriestly Prayer" seems a fitting conclusion. Jesus' prayer at the Last Supper—that the unity of his apostles and of his Church should mirror the unity within the Trinity—is intimately linked to, and will be effected by, this great unifying sacrament.

ACKNOWLEDGMENTS

The Publisher wishes to acknowledge the use of copyright material reprinted by permission of the following:

The three New Testament quotations from the first chapter are taken from the *Lectionary for Mass for Use in the Dioceses of the United States of America,* second typical edition © 2001, 1998, 1997, 1970, Confraternity of Christian Doctrine, Inc., Washington, DC. Used with permission. All rights reserved. No portion of this text may be reproduced by any means without permission in writing from the copyright owner.

The selection from St. Nicholas Cabasilas is taken from *A Word in Season,* vol. 3, Easter. Years I and II (Villanova, PA: Augustinian Press, 2001), 210–11.

Passages from *The Imitation of Christ* by Thomas à Kempis are taken from the Ronald Knox/Michael Oakley translation. Permission granted by Ignatius Press, San Francisco.

The hymn "Weave a Song within the Silence" was originally published in the *Hymnal for the Hours.* Copyright © 1989 by GIA Publications, Inc., Chicago, IL 60638. All Rights Reserved. Used by permission.

"The Highpriestly Prayer" was originally published as "Jesus' Prayer for the Church." The International Commission on English, *Liturgy, Resource Collection,* 1981. Revised and used with permission.

The following poems originally appeared in the publications listed below:

"My Peace" and "The Hands of Christ" in *Ripples of Stillness,* ©1978

Ralph Wright, OSB. Pauline Books and Media, Boston: St. Paul Editions.

"Messiah" and "Unless a Grain" in *Life is Simpler Towards Evening* (The Golden Quill Press, 1983).

"Antioch," "The Body of Christ," "The Way is Hard," and "Unsurprised by Darkness" in *Seamless* (The Golden Quill, 1992).

"Pivotal" and "Learn From Me" in *Christ, Our Love for All Seasons* (Paulist Press, 2005).

The hymn "The Word Became in Jesus" was first published in *Praise the Lord* (London: Geoffrey Chapman, 1972). The version printed here has been revised.

Besides Fr. Laurence Kriegshauser to whom this book is dedicated, I would like to thank Abbot Thomas Frerking and the monk priests of Saint Louis Abbey from whose homilies over the years I have received wisdom and understanding that have deepened my appreciation of our daily bread. I would also like to thank Br. Philip O'Donnell whose help once again in meticulously proofing the text has been invaluable.

Ralph Wright, OSB
August 2007

INTRODUCTION

Pope John Paul II's encyclical *Ecclesia de Eucharistia* (2003) opened new doors onto the mystery of the Eucharist. It seems likely that the pope conceived the idea of this encyclical when, in 2000, he celebrated Holy Thursday in the Cenacle in Jerusalem, where tradition says Jesus celebrated the first Eucharist. How was it possible that this event could have happened before Jesus had died on Calvary on the first Good Friday? How was it possible that the disciples at that first Eucharist received the identical Body and Blood of the Lord that we now receive each time we go to communion? *This* is the mystery that John Paul, philosopher as he was, set out to throw new light on. To do so he used the Italian abstract noun *contemporaneità*. The English translators did not hazard an equivalent, such as venturing to use a verb like *contemporize,* and instead used "oneness in time." However, my own literal translation of the Italian might be "[Jesus] instituted a mysterious contemporaneousness between the Paschal Triduum and the flow of the centuries."[1]

The Eucharist, Pope John Paul II might have said, makes us contemporary with the Paschal Triduum. The mystery of the Eucharist is that it takes the "event" of the three-day Triduum—like the "event" of a German sentence with the verb at the end—and lifts it out of time so that it can be re-actualized at every Eucharist from Holy Thursday till the end of time. It is like a recording being replayed, only in this case it is the reality itself that is being re-actualized, and not the sound or vision of the event captured on tape or digital and being "replayed."

Christ did this so that, for the rest of human history, those who believe in him and are baptized "into him"—those who are trying to live his life—*might be able to be present at the Triduum* and be able to offer, with Jesus, the supreme sacrifice of their lives to the Father for the permanent reunion of humankind with the Holy Trinity, whose love for each individual person is the reason for the whole drama of humanity on earth.

The "amazingness" of all this—that John Paul hopes will fill every minister of the Eucharist, and every person celebrating with him—is what I began to feel as I read that part of his encyclical and attempted to share it with others. There can be no greater action that a human being can perform than this. At the culmination of the Eucharistic prayer the priest raises on high the paten with the hosts upon it and the chalice with the precious blood contained within it and says: "Through Him, with Him, in Him, in the unity of the Holy Spirit, all glory and honor is yours, Almighty Father, for ever and ever." And the congregation responds: "Amen."

It is at this moment that each person offers him- or herself— with all their achievements and failures, all their humility and arrogance—together with Jesus to the heavenly Father. Each day is the repetition of our redemption, each day the complete Triduum— from the last supper to the meeting with Mary Magdalen beside the empty tomb. Whether it is Justin Martyr describing the Sunday Liturgy of second-century Christians; Thomas à Kempis from the fifteenth century praising a God who loves us so much that he nourishes souls with himself; twentieth-century Fr. Alfred Delp, two days before his execution by the Gestapo, writing that there was no difference saying Mass in his narrow cell than anywhere else; or twenty-first century Pope Benedict XVI saying Mass before millions of young people on World Youth Day—whichever it is, across the centuries, it is the identical mystery that is being celebrated.

FIRST CENTURY

ST. PAUL
ST. MARK
ST. JOHN

～◦～

O the Mystery Unfathomable

O the mystery unfathomable
That the one who is our God
Through the grape and through the grain
Should have deigned to be our food.
Now the greatness of his nature
Lies so humbly here revealed
That the splendor of a billion stars
So completely had concealed.

For our God who is perfection,
Three persons who are one,
From eternity being happy,
Having all and needing none,
Freely chose to breathe creation
Like a breath upon a pane
And so started the long journey
Towards the bread and towards the wine.

Aeons later out of darkness
From a star that had gone cold
Rose the wonder of the life forms

That would fill a waking world.
Like a nest prepared by instinct
By the female for her brood
So the world through many ages
Wove a womb to nestle God.

Till in Mary who was perfect
Undisturbed by any ill,
Was a woman now created
Who would choose to do God's will.
Here at last was one whose person
Was so simple and so pure
That the Lord of all creation
In her womb could be secure.

So he came—in whom all nature
Every star and every world
Has its being—to be with us
In the womb of this young girl.
So he came to walk among us
For a flash of thirty years,
Like a word into our silence,
Like a hope against our fears.

O how deeply was he woven
In the fibers of our flesh,
Within Mary through the Spirit
God embraced the human mesh.
Like the wool upon the needles,
Like the garment on the loom,
So our God became our Jesus
In the darkness of the womb.

Thirty years he worked in silence
As a carpenter at home,
Then he told us of his Father
As whose envoy he had come.
Though he healed us and forgave us
He confronted all our pride

Then he gently bore our insults,
And we nailed him and he died.

But before his life was ended
By the ones whom he had loved
He conceived a way to weave us
To his body and his blood.
While at supper that last evening
On the night before he died
Through the bread and through the wine cup
He became our very food.

O the mystery unfathomable
That the one who is our God
Through the grape and through the grain
Should have deigned to be our food.
Now the greatness of his nature
Lies so humbly here revealed
That the splendor of a billion stars
So completely had concealed.

St. Paul

The first Eucharist described

I received from the Lord what I also handed on to you, that the Lord Jesus, on the night he was handed over, took bread, and, after he had given thanks, broke it and said, "This is my Body that is for you. Do this in remembrance of me." In the same way also the cup, after supper, saying, "This cup is the new covenant in my Blood. Do this, as often as you drink it, in remembrance of me."

For as often as you eat this bread and drink the cup, you proclaim the death of the Lord until he comes. (1 Cor 11:23–26)

St. Mark

The first Gospel account of the Eucharist

While they were eating, he took bread, said the blessing, broke it and gave it to them, and said, "Take it; this is my Body." Then he took a cup, gave thanks, and gave it to them, and they all drank from it. He said to them, "This is my Blood of the covenant, which will be shed for many. Amen, I say to you, I shall not drink again the fruit of the vine until the day when I drink it new in the Kingdom of God." (Mark 14:22–25)

St. John

The Bread of Life

Jesus said to the crowds: "Amen, amen, I say to you, unless you eat the Flesh of the Son of Man and drink his Blood, you do not have life within you. Whoever eats my Flesh and drinks my Blood has eternal life, and I will raise him on the last day. For my Flesh is true food, and my Blood is true drink. Whoever eats my Flesh and drinks my Blood remains in me and I in him. Just as the living Father sent me and I have life because of the Father, so also the one who feeds on me will have life because of me. This is the bread that came down from heaven. Unlike your ancestors who ate and still died, whoever eats this bread will live forever." (John 6:53–58)

SECOND CENTURY

ST. IGNATIUS OF ANTIOCH
ST. JUSTIN
TERTULLIAN

Antioch

Ignatius longed
to be wheat
ground pure
by the teeth of beasts
to become the strong
bread of life
fed to his brothers
the Body of Christ

Was he glad
to be scourged pure
when the tongues of men
lashed him raw
when his grain was broken
his grape trod
and he was used
for the Body of God?

St. Ignatius of Antioch

St. Ignatius was born in Syria about the year 50 and died in Rome between 98 and 117. Like his friend St. Polycarp, he may have personally heard the preaching of St. John the Evangelist. According to St. John Chrysostom, he received episcopal ordination at the hands of the apostles themselves. He was condemned under Emperor Trajan. On his way to Rome to meet the wild beasts, he wrote letters to the churches in Ephesus, Magnesia, Trales, and Smyrna. The letters reveal his dynamic faith, his eagerness to die as a martyr, and the deep love he had for the Eucharist, which must, he wrote, always be celebrated in union with the local bishop.[2]

LETTER TO THE SMYRNAEANS

The Eucharist is the flesh of our Savior.

6. Let no one's position puff him up; for faith and charity are all in all, and nothing is to be preferred to them. Consider how contrary to the mind of God are the heterodox in regard to the grace of God which has come to us. They have no regard for charity, none for the widow, the orphan, the oppressed, none for the man in prison, the hungry or the thirsty. They abstain from the Eucharist and from prayer because they do not admit that the Eucharist is the flesh of our Savior Jesus Christ, the flesh which suffered for our sins and which the Father, in His graciousness, raised from the dead.

LETTER TO THE ROMANS

Love that cannot be destroyed

7. The prince of this world is eager to tear me to pieces, to weaken my will that is fixed on God. Let none of you who are watching the battle abet him. Come in rather on my side, for it is the side of God. Do not let your lips be for Jesus Christ and your heart for the world. Let envy have no place among you. And even, when I am come, if I should beseech you, pay no attention to what I say; believe, rather, what I am writing to you now. For alive as I am at this moment of writing, my longing is for death. Desire with me has been nailed to the cross and no flame of material longing is

left. Only the living water speaks within me saying: Hasten to the Father. I have no taste for the food that perishes nor for the pleasures of this life. I want the Bread of God which is the Flesh of Christ, who was of the seed of David; and for drink I desire His blood which is love that cannot be destroyed.

ST. JUSTIN

In what had once been Samaria, Justin Martyr was born of pagan parents around 100 and died as a martyr in 165. After an education in Greek philosophy he came via Judaism to Christianity. He then became a promoter and defender of the Christian faith. In his First Apology *he tried to show Emperor Antoninus Pius that it was immoral to kill Christians who were good citizens just because they believed in Christ. He warned the emperor that killing the just unjustly would lead to eternal punishment after death while those he was executing would go straight to Christ. He also gave the first account of a Sunday liturgy.*[3]

FIRST APOLOGY

The first account of a Sunday liturgy

66. We call this food the Eucharist, of which only he can partake who has acknowledged the truth of our teachings, who has been cleansed by baptism for the remission of his sins and for his regeneration, and who regulates his life upon the principles laid down by Christ. Not as ordinary bread or as ordinary drink do we partake of them, but just as, through the word of God, our Savior Jesus Christ became incarnate and took upon Himself flesh and blood for our salvation, so, we have been taught, the food which has been made the Eucharist by the prayer of His word, and which nourishes our flesh and blood by assimilation, is both the flesh and blood of that Jesus who was made flesh. The Apostles in their memoirs, which are called gospels, have handed down what Jesus ordered them to do; that he took bread and, after giving thanks, said: "Do this in remembrance of Me; this is My body." In like manner, He took also the chalice, gave thanks and said: "This is My blood"; and to them only did He give it."

67. On the day which is called Sunday we have a common assembly of all who live in the cities or in the outlying districts, and the memoirs of the Apostles or the writings of the Prophets are read, as long as there is time. Then, when the reader has finished, the president of the assembly admonishes and invites all to imitate such examples of virtue. Then we all stand up together and offer up our prayers, and, as we said before, after we finish our prayers, bread and wine and water are presented. He who presides likewise offers up prayers and thanksgivings, to the best of his ability, and the people express their approval by saying "Amen." The Eucharistic elements are distributed and consumed by those present, and to those who are absent they are sent through the deacons. The wealthy, if they wish, contribute whatever they desire, and the collection is placed in the custody of the president. With it he helps the orphans and widows, those who are needy because of sickness or any other reason, and the captives and strangers in our midst; in short, he takes care of all those in need. Sunday, indeed, is the day on which we all hold our common assembly because it is the first day on which God, transforming the darkness and prime matter, created the world; and our Savior Jesus Christ arose from the dead on the same day. For they crucified him on the day before that of Saturn, and on the day after, which is Sunday, He appeared to His Apostles and disciples, and taught them the things which we have passed on to you also for consideration.

TERTULLIAN

Tertullian was born in Carthage in 160. The son of a centurion, he was by profession an advocate. He converted around 197 and seems to have been ordained a priest about the year 200, but left the Church to become a Montanist around 206. While still a Catholic he wrote the treatise "On Prayer," which included a commentary on the Our Father, which he called a "compendium of the whole Gospel." A memorable statement of his concerning the Eucharist says: "The flesh feeds on the body and blood of Christ that the soul may be sated with God."[4] Tertullian died around 220.

ON PRAYER

Our "daily bread"—Christ

6. With what exquisite choice has divine Wisdom arranged the order of [the Our Father] that, after the matters which pertain to heaven—that is after the name of God, the will of God and the kingdom of God—it should make a place for a petition for our earthly needs, too? For our Lord has taught us: "Seek first the kingdom, and then these things shall be given you besides." However, we should rather understand "Give us this day our daily bread" in a spiritual sense. For Christ is "our bread," because Christ is Life and the Life is Bread. "I am," said He, "the bread of life." And shortly before: "The bread is the word of the living God who hath come down from heaven." Then, because His Body is considered to be in the bread: "This is my body." Therefore, when we ask for our daily bread, we are asking to live forever in Christ and to be inseparably united with His Body.

THIRD CENTURY

ST. CYPRIAN
ST. EUSEBIUS OF CAESAREA

Messiah

anoint the wounds
of my spirit
with the balm
of forgiveness
pour the oil
of your calm
on the waters
of my heart

take the squeal
of frustration
from the wheels
of my passion
that the power
of your tenderness
may smooth
the way I love

that the tedium
of giving
in the risk
of surrender

and the reaching
out naked
to a world
that must wound

may be kindled
fresh daily
to a blaze
of compassion
that the grain
may fall gladly
to burst in the ground
—and the harvest abound

St. Cyprian

Born around 200, Cyprian was a rhetorician who was converted to Christianity about 245 and was elected bishop of Carthage in 248. The Decian persecution broke out in 249, so he went into hiding and used letters to stay in touch with his people. When the persecution ended, he got embroiled with the controversy about the reconciliation of those who had lapsed, and later with the validity of the baptism of schismatics. His treatise on the unity of the Church and his letter on the Eucharist are still inspiring and enlightening. He died in Carthage a martyr in the Valerian persecution in 258.[5]

TREATISE 4

Praying so as not to fall into a sin that might separate us from Christ's body

18. As the [Our Father] proceeds, we ask and say: "Give us this day our daily bread." This can be understood both spiritually and simply, because either understanding is of profit in divine usefulness for salvation. For Christ is the bread of life and the bread here is of all, but is ours. And as we say "Our Father," because He is the Father of those who understand and believe, so too we say "our Bread," because Christ is the bread of those who attain to His body. Moreover, we ask that this bread be given daily, lest we, who are in Christ and receive the Eucharist daily as food of salvation, with the intervention of some more grievous sin, while we are shut off and as non-communicants are kept from the heavenly bread, be separated from the body of Christ as He Himself declares, saying: "I am the bread of life which came down from heaven. If any man eat of my bread he shall live forever. Moreover, the bread that I shall give is my flesh for the life of the world." Since then He says that, if anyone eats of His bread, he lives forever, as it is manifest that they live who attain to His body and receive the Eucharist by right of communion, so on the other hand we must fear and pray lest anyone, while he is cut off and separated from the body of Christ, remain apart from salvation, as He Himself threatens saying: "Unless you eat the flesh of the Son of man and drink His blood, you shall not have life in you." And so we petition that our bread, that is Christ,

be given us daily, so that we, who abide and live in Christ, may not withdraw from His sanctification and body.

St. Eusebius of Caesarea

Eusebius was born in about 260 and died about 340. In 313 he became bishop of Caesarea. He sided with Arius in the early stages of this heresy, but at the Council of Nicaea he was reinstated by Constantine. He is known as the "Father of Church History," recording what had happened from Jesus' day down to his own. Critical historians distrust his judgment but he seemed to have had a vivid awareness of how much "history" exists in the precarious oral tradition of eyewitnesses and so made it his business to record as much as he could while eyewitnesses were still around.[6]

SUNDAY EUCHARIST

The new Passover celebrated each Sunday

In the time of Moses the paschal lamb was sacrificed only once a year, on the fourteenth day of the first month towards evening, but we of the new covenant celebrate our Passover every week on the Lord's day. We are continually being filled with the body of the Savior and sharing in the blood of the Lamb. Daily we gird ourselves with chastity and prepare, staff in hand, to follow the path of the gospel. Leaning on the rod that came forth from the root of Jesse, we are always departing from Egypt in search of the solitude of the desert. We are constantly setting out on our journey to God and celebrating the Passover. The gospel would have us do these things not only once a year but daily....

On the fifth day of the week, while having supper with his disciples, the Savior said to them: *With all my heart I have longed to eat this Passover with you.* It was not the old Jewish Passover that he desired to share with his disciples, but the new Passover of the new covenant that he was giving them, and that many prophets and upright people before him had longed to see. He proclaimed his desire for the new Passover which he, the Word himself, in his infinite thirst for the salvation of the whole human race, was establishing as a feast to be celebrated by all peoples everywhere. The

Passover of Moses was not for all peoples, indeed it could not be, because the law allowed it to be celebrated only in Jerusalem. Christ's desire, then, must have been not for that old Passover, but for the saving mystery of the new covenant which was for everyone.

And so we too should eat this Passover with Christ. We should cleanse our minds of all the leaven of evil and wickedness and be filled with the unleavened bread of sincerity and truth, becoming Jews inwardly, in our souls, where the true circumcision takes place. We should anoint the lintel of our mind with the blood of the Lamb who was sacrificed for us, and so ward off our destroyer. We should do this not only once a year, but every week, continually.

On the day before the Sabbath we fast in memory of our Savior's passion, as the apostles were the first to do when the bridegroom was taken from them. On the Lord's day we receive life from the sacred body of our saving Passover and our souls are sealed with his precious blood.

FOURTH CENTURY

ST. CYRIL OF JERUSALEM
ST. AMBROSE
ST. JOHN CHRYSOSTOM
ST. AUGUSTINE OF HIPPO
ABBOT JOHN CASSIAN

Man holds

Man holds
within his hand
the one who holds
within his hand
the universe—
cup your hand in awe, O Man,
and pray
that He who comes so humbly
unto you
as food
may make you worthy of himself
eternally
as God.

St. Cyril of Jerusalem

Cyril was born in 315. He became bishop of Jerusalem about 348. The Arian heresy was strong then and he was driven into exile several times. He is famous for his Catechetical Lectures. He stressed the presence of the Lord in the Eucharist, writing "Not of this Bread is it said that 'It passes into the stomach and so is discharged into the drain'; no, it is absorbed into your whole system to the benefit of both soul and body."[7] He died in 386.

MYSTAGOGICAL LECTURE 4

The senses see the bread and wine. Faith sees the Body of Christ.

2. Once at Cana in Galilee He changed water into wine by His sovereign will; is it not credible, then, that He changed wine into his blood? If as a guest at a physical marriage He performed this stupendous miracle, shall He not far more readily be confessed to have bestowed on "the friends of the bridegroom" the fruition of His own Body and Blood?

3. With perfect confidence, then, we partake as of the Body and Blood of Christ. For in the figure of bread His Body is given to you, and in the figure of wine His Blood, that by partaking of the Body and Blood of Christ you may become of one body and blood with Him. For when His Body and Blood become the tissue of our members, we become Christ-bearers and as the blessed Peter said, "partakers of the divine nature."

4. Once, speaking to the Jews, Christ said: "Unless you eat my flesh and drink my blood, you can have no life in you." Not understanding His words spiritually, they "were shocked and drew back," imagining that He was proposing the eating of human flesh.

5. The Old Covenant had its loaves of proposition, but they, as belonging to the Covenant, have come to an end. The New Covenant has its heavenly bread and cup of salvation, to sanctify both body and soul. For as the bread is for the body, the Word suits the soul.

6. Do not then think of the elements as bare bread and wine; they are, according to the Lord's declaration, the Body and Blood of Christ. Though sense suggests the contrary, let faith be your stay. Instead of judging the matter by taste, let faith give you an unwa-

vering confidence that you have been privileged to receive the Body and Blood of Christ.

ST. AMBROSE

St. Ambrose was born in Trier around 339. His father was the praetorian prefect of Gaul. When the Arian bishop of Milan died in 373, Ambrose was ensuring order for the election of a successor when someone cried out: "Ambrose for bishop!" Chosen by popular acclaim, even though still a catechumen, he was baptized, ordained, consecrated, and installed. He became an outstanding preacher and a staunch opponent of Arianism. Ambrose's preaching had a profound influence on the young Augustine (later bishop of Hippo) and helped lead to his conversion. Ambrose died in 397.[8]

THE SACRAMENTS

We need the Eucharist daily for the wound of our sinfulness.

21. Do you wish to know how [the bread] is consecrated with heavenly words? Accept what the words are. The priest speaks. He says: "Perform for us this oblation written, reasonable, acceptable, which is a figure of the body and blood of our Lord Jesus Christ. On the day before He suffered He took bread in His holy hands, looked toward heaven, toward you, holy Father omnipotent, eternal God, giving thanks, blessed, broke, and having broken it gave it to the Apostles and His disciples, saying: 'Take and eat of this, all of you; for this is my body, which shall be broken for many.'" Take note.

22. "Similarly also, on the day before He suffered, after they had dined, He took the chalice, looked toward heaven, toward thee, holy Father omnipotent, eternal God and giving thanks He blessed it, and gave it to the Apostles and His disciples, saying: 'Take and drink of this, all of you; for this is my blood.'" Behold! All these words up to "Take" are the Evangelist's, whether body or blood. From then on the words are Christ's: "Take and drink of this, all of you; for this is my blood."

23. Look at these events one by one. It says: "On the day before He suffered, He took bread in His holy hands." Before it is

consecrated, it is bread; but when Christ's words have been added, it is the body of Christ. Finally, hear him as He says: "Take and eat of this all of you; for this is my body." And before the words of Christ, the chalice is full of wine and water; when the words of Christ have been added, then blood is effected, which redeemed the people. So behold in what great respects the expression of Christ is able to change all things. Then the Lord Jesus Himself testified to us that we receive His body and blood. Should we doubt at all about His faith and testimony?

24. Now return with me to my proposition. Great and venerable indeed is the fact that manna rained upon the Jews from heaven. But understand! What is greater, manna from heaven or the body of Christ? Surely the body of Christ, who is the Author of heaven. Then, he who ate the manna died; he who has eaten this body will effect for himself remission of sins and "shall not die forever."

"Give us this day our daily bread." If bread is daily, why do you take it after a year, as the Greeks in the East are accustomed to do? Receive daily what is of benefit to you daily! So live that you may deserve to receive it daily! He who does not deserve to receive it daily does not deserve to receive it after a year. In this manner holy Job offered sacrifice for his sons daily, lest, perchance, they had committed some sin either in heart or speech. Then do you hear that, as often as the sacrifice is offered, the death of the Lord, the resurrection of the Lord, the elevation of the Lord, is signified, and the remission of sins, and do you not take this bread of life daily? He who has a wound requires medicine. The fact that we are under sin is a wound; the medicine is the heavenly and venerable sacrament.

St. John Chrysostom

John Chrysostom was born in Antioch around 347. From roughly 373–381 he lived a monastic life at his home under the Rule of St. Pachomius. He was ordained priest in 386. He directed his sermons to the moral reform of the Christians of his day, and his excellent preaching won him his nickname "Goldenmouthed." His commentaries and homilies on holy scripture combine spiritual insight with practical suggestions about living the Gospel. In 398 he was made patriarch of Constantinople but blunt criticism of the Empress Eudoxia and her wild court life led to his exile. He died in the region of Pontus in 407.[9]

HOMILY 24: ON FIRST CORINTHIANS

We behold in the Eucharist the one who is beheld in heaven.

7. Christ gave us his flesh to eat in order to deepen our love for him. When we approach him there should be burning within us a fire of love and longing.

8. This food strengthens us; it emboldens us to speak freely to our God; it is our hope, our salvation, our light and our life. If we go to the next world fortified by this sacrifice, we shall enter its sacred portals with perfect confidence, as though protected all over by armor of gold.

But why do I speak of the next world? Because of this sacrament earth becomes heaven for you. Throw open the gates of heaven—or rather, not of heaven, but of the heaven of heavens— look through and you will see the proof of what I say. What is heaven's most precious possession? I will show you it here on earth. I do not show you angels or archangels, heaven or the heaven of heavens, but I show you the very Lord of all these. Do you not see how you gaze, here on earth, upon what is most precious of all? You not only gaze on it but touch it as well. You not only touch it, but even eat it and take it away with you to your homes. It is essential therefore when you wish to receive this sacrament to cleanse your soul from sin and to prepare your mind.

ST. AUGUSTINE OF HIPPO

Augustine of Hippo was born in Thagaste, Algeria, in 354—his father a pagan, his mother, St. Monica, a Christian. He had a long search for meaning and happiness, drinking deep of the pleasures that life offered. His mother's prayers, Neoplatonism, St. Ambrose—all played a role in his conversion in 387. Returning to Africa he was ordained priest in 391 and acclaimed bishop of Hippo in 395. Confronting Pelagianism, Augustine taught that grace is needed for us to extricate ourselves from the mire of original sin and embrace God's love made visible in Jesus. Under grace, "Love and do what you will!" can become our motto.[10] *He died in 430.*

SERMON 272

Sacrament: called so because our eyes see one thing, our understanding (through faith) another

You see, on God's altar, bread and a cup. That is what the evidence of your eyes tells you, but your faith requires you to believe that the bread is the body of Christ, the cup the blood of Christ. In these few words we can say perhaps all that faith demands.

Faith, however, seeks understanding; so you may now say to me: "You have told us what we have to believe, but explain it so that we can understand it, because it is quite possible for someone to think along these lines: We know from whom our Lord Jesus Christ took his flesh—it was from the Virgin Mary. As a baby, he was suckled, he was fed, he developed, he came to a young man's estate. He was slain on the cross, he was taken down from it, he was buried, he rose again on the third day. On the day of his own choosing, he ascended to heaven, taking his body with him; and it is from heaven that he will come to judge the living and the dead. But now that he is there, seated at the right hand of the Father, how can bread be his body? And the cup, or rather what is in the cup, how can that be his blood?"

These things, my friends, are called sacraments, because our eyes see in them one thing, our understanding another. Our eyes see the material form; our understanding, its spiritual effect. If, then, you want to know what the body of Christ is, you must listen to what the Apostle tells the faithful: *Now you are the body of Christ, and individually you are members of it.*

If that is so, it is the sacrament of yourselves that is placed on the Lord's altar, and it is the sacrament of yourselves that you receive. You reply "Amen" to what you are, and thereby agree that such you are. You hear the words "The body of Christ" and you reply "Amen." Be, then, a member of Christ's body, so that your "Amen" may accord with the truth.

ABBOT JOHN CASSIAN

Abbot John Cassian was born in Scythia in 360. He spent some fifteen years in Egypt researching the monks' lives, and there was a disciple of Evagrius Ponticus. In 415 he founded two monasteries near Marseilles. In the Institutes he prescribes rules to cope with the vices that prevent our union with God. In the Conferences, *which is wisdom distilled from his time in Egypt, he invites us to "look with a kind of overwhelming wonder at (God's) ineffable gentleness." What we can see of God depends on "the character of our life and the purity of our heart"(1.XV.1). St. Benedict learned much from his writings. Cassian died in Marseilles in 435.*[11]

NINTH CONFERENCE: ON PRAYER

We are unable to attain a spiritual life without the Eucharist.

XXI.1. Then: "Give us this day our supersubstantial 'bread'" which another evangelist has referred to as "daily." The former indicates the noble quality of this substance, which places it above all other substances and which in the sublimity of its magnificence and power to sanctify surpasses every creature, whereas the latter expresses the nature of its use and its goodness. For when it says "daily" it shows that we are unable to attain the spiritual life on a day without it.

XXI.2. When it says "this day" it shows that it must be taken daily and that yesterday's supply of it is not enough if we have not been given of it today as well. Our daily need for it warns us that we should pour out this prayer constantly, because there is no day on which it is not necessary for us to strengthen the heart of our inner man by eating and receiving this. But the expression "this day" can also be understood with reference to the present life—namely: Give us this bread as long as we dwell in this world. For we know that it will also be given in the world to come to those who have deserved it from you, but we beg you to give it to us this day, because unless a person deserves to receive it in this life he will be unable to partake of it in that life.

FIFTH CENTURY

ST. PETER CHRYSOLOGUS

The Way Is Hard

the Way is hard
long winding narrow
—sometimes steep—
through woods valleys
mountains deserts
"a lifetime's march"
while the World whispers
to hungry hearts
"turn these stones to bread"

but the Word coming
from the mouth of God
says "if a child
ask his father
for a loaf of bread
will he give him a stone?
I tell you this
that my joy
may be in you:
I and the Father are one"

they take up stones
to silence him
but he passes

through their midst
later they come
and he stands still
to let the grain
be harvested

taken pounded
ground to powder
yeasted kneaded
baked and offered
as food sufficient
for a day's march
—the Way is hard—
come take and eat
that your joy too
may be complete

St. Peter Chrysologus

Peter Chrysologus was born in Aemilia around 400. While still a deacon he was appointed archbishop of Ravenna. His preaching inspired his people to imitate Christ. Attacking error, he explained the Catholic teaching on the Incarnation, on grace, and on the Virgin birth. Nicknamed "Goldenworded" because of his eloquence, he wrote of the returning prodigal son "'When he was still a long way off his father saw him' ...Night buries yesterday's daylight. Sin removes vision....If the heavenly father had not removed by the light of his glance all the darkness of his confusion, the son would never have seen the brightness of the divine face" (Sermon 3 on Luke 15:20–24).[12] He died in 450.

SERMON 67 ON THE LORD'S PRAYER (MATT 6:9–13)

He is the bread who daily supplies heavenly food to the faithful.

Give us this day our daily bread. He who gave himself to us as a Father, who adopted us as his sons, who made us heirs of everything, who ennobled us with a name, who both gave us his own honors and his own Kingdom, does he assign us the task of asking for our daily bread? In the Kingdom of God is this what human poverty seeks out among the divine gifts? Does this good Father, this pious Father, this generous Father have to be asked before he will give his sons bread? And how is this compatible with the text: "Do not be anxious about what you are to eat, or what you are to drink or how you are to be clothed?" (Matt. 6) Is he instructing them here to ask for what elsewhere he forbade them even to think about? Isn't it rather that as their heavenly Father he is asking them as heavenly sons to ask for the heavenly bread? He himself said "I am the Bread that came down from heaven." (Jn. 6) He himself is the bread that was sown in the virgin, yeasted in the flesh, kneaded in his passion, baked in the oven of the tomb, stored in the Churches, brought to the altars and daily provides heavenly food for the faithful.

And forgive us our trespasses. As we forgive those who trespass against us. Man, if you cannot be without sin, and want to be always

---

totally forgiven, then always forgive. Forgive with the same measure with which you wish to be forgiven—forgive as often as you wish to be forgiven and since in fact you want to be forgiven totally, forgive totally. Realize, Man, that by forgiving others you are winning pardon for yourself.

SIXTH CENTURY

ST. GREGORY THE GREAT

Since Babel God

Since Babel God
spoke haltingly
through prophets
(whom we killed)
down to our own
sweet day

when
to avoid
the ambiguities
of language
God sent in flesh his Son

this flesh
we nailed
like incoherence
to a tree

but he
rose to win us wholeness
making all twos one
unbabeling our language
in the blood of union

St. Gregory the Great

Gregory the Great was born in Rome in 540, the son of a senator. Educated in law, he was made prefect of the city, developing thereby his skills as an administrator. He sold his property and became a monk in the monastery he founded on the Celian Hill. He was ambassador in Constantinople for six years, then abbot, then deacon, and then, reluctantly, pope. Italy was in chaos—war, plague, flooding, disorder, poverty. With strength, vision, and gentleness, he brought order to the city and the Church. He made peace, reformed the liturgy, wrote a handbook for bishops on the care of souls, and kept his monastic simplicity.[13] He died in 604.

THE DIALOGUES, BOOK 4

Mass offered for those in purgatory

59. The benefits of the holy Sacrifice are only for those who, by their good lives, have merited the grace of receiving help from the good deeds others perform in their behalf.

60. The safer course, naturally, is to do for ourselves during life what we hope others will do for us after death. It is better to make one's exit a free man than to seek liberty after one is in chains. We should, therefore, despise this world with all our hearts as though its glory were already spent, and offer our sacrifice of tears to God each day as we immolate His sacred Flesh and Blood. This Sacrifice alone has the power of saving the soul from eternal death, for it presents to us mystically the death of the only-begotten Son. Though He is now risen from the dead and dies no more, and "death has no more power over him," yet, living in Himself immortal and incorruptible, He is again immolated for us in the mystery of the holy Sacrifice. Where his Body is eaten, there His Flesh is distributed among the people for their salvation. His Blood no longer stains the hands of the godless, but flows into the hearts of His faithful followers. See, then, how august the Sacrifice that is offered for us, ever reproducing in itself the passion of the only-begotten Son for the remission of our sins. For, who of the faithful can have any doubt that at the moment of the immolation, at the

sound of the priest's voice, the heavens stand open and choirs of angels are present at the mystery of Jesus Christ. There at the altar the lowliest is united with the most sublime, earth is joined with heaven, the visible and invisible somehow merge into one.

SEVENTH CENTURY

ST. JOHN DAMASCENE

The Word Became in Jesus

The Word became in Jesus
A man though being God
That he might touch and heal us
With hands of flesh and blood.

We took the gifts he brought us
And found that they were good,
Then took the hands that brought them
And nailed them down to wood.

But God in his great wisdom
Through love had found a way
To be with us for ever—
The grain that died would stay.

His love became Christ Jesus,
His life becomes our food;
Through bread and wine we feed on
The very life of God.

O sing of praise and wonder
May joy fill every phrase,
His Word become our life blood
Will sing through us God's praise.

St. John Damascene

John of Damascus, or John Damascene, was born to a wealthy, leading Christian in Damascus in 657. All of his life was spent under Muslim rule. In 716 he became a monk at St. Saba near Jerusalem, where he wrote poetry and theology until his death in 749. His greatest theological work was The Fount of Wisdom. *Parts 1 and 2 of this work deal with philosophy and heresy; in Part 3, "Exposition on the Orthodox Faith," he synthesized the teaching of the Greek Fathers on the central mysteries of the Christian faith: the Incarnation, the Trinity, and the Eucharist.*[14]

EXPOSITION OF THE ORTHODOX FAITH, BOOK 4

How do bread and wine become at the consecration the Body and Blood of Christ? Through the Holy Spirit.

13. Further, bread and wine are employed: for God knoweth man's infirmity: for in general man turns away discontentedly from what is not well-worn by custom: and so with [God's] usual indulgence He performs His supernatural works through familiar objects: and just as, in the case of baptism, since it is man's custom to wash himself with water and anoint himself with oil, He connected the grace of the Spirit with the oil and the water and made it the water of regeneration, in like manner since it is man's custom to eat and drink water and wine, He connected His divinity with these and made them His body and blood in order that we may rise to what is supernatural through what is familiar and natural.

The body which is born of the holy Virgin is in truth body united with divinity, not that the body which was received up into the heavens descends, but that the bread itself and the wine are changed into God's body and blood. But if you enquire how this happens, it is enough to learn that it was through the Holy Spirit, just as the Lord Himself took on Himself flesh that subsisted in Him and was born of the holy Mother of God through the Spirit. And we know nothing further save that the Word of God is true and energizes and is omnipotent, but the manner of this cannot be searched out. But one can put it well thus, that just as in nature the bread by eating and the wine and water by drinking are changed into the body and blood of the eater and drinker, and do not become a different body from the former one, so the bread of the table and the wine and water are supernaturally changed by the invocation and presence of the Holy Spirit into the body and blood of Christ, and are not two but one and the same.

The bread and wine are not merely figures of the body and blood of Christ (God forbid!) but the deified body of the Lord itself: for the Lord has said, "This is My body," not, this is a figure of My body; and "My blood," not, a figure of My blood. And on a previous occasion He had said to the Jews, *Except ye eat the flesh of the son of Man and drink His blood, ye have no life in you. For My flesh is meat indeed and My blood is drink indeed.* And again, *He that eateth Me, shall live.*

Wherefore with all fear and a pure conscience and certain faith let us draw near and it will assuredly be to us as we believe, doubting nothing. Let us pay homage to it in all purity both of soul and body: for it is twofold. Let us draw near to it with an ardent desire, and with our hands held in the form of a cross let us receive the body of the Crucified One: and let us apply our eyes and lips and brows and partake of the divine coal, in order that the fire of the longing, that is in us, with the additional heat derived from the coal may utterly consume our sins and illumine our hearts, and that we may be inflamed and deified by the participation in the divine fire.

EIGHTH CENTURY

ST. BEDE THE VENERABLE

Unsurprised by Darkness

if God's own Son
had to brink despair
dying in the darkness
of noonday night

why should I
know a tranquil passage
from finite groping
to infinite Light

why am I shocked
by the daily trauma
woven into
the heart of flesh

the rending anger
perdures from the womb
till the hands are folded
in the calm of death

see the stars
and ponder the Word
in whom each galaxy
finds its being

then watch the one
whose humble coming
respects the measure
of our seeing

for "who can live
with a blazing fire?"
O mercifully mercifully
hidden God

coming as breeze
coming as bread
coming through the grape
our feet have trod

St. Bede the Venerable

Born in 673, St. Bede was brought at age seven to England, first to the monastery at Wearmouth and then to the "co-monastery" at Jarrow when that was founded in 682. Here he lived the ordinary life of a monk until his death in 735. Ordained deacon at nineteen and priest at thirty, he was a scholar, exegete, and historian. His Ecclesiastical History of the English People is crucial for our knowledge of early England, and his scriptural exegesis is often invigorating: "Why man are you proud? God on your behalf has become humble. You would perhaps be ashamed to imitate a humble man, at least imitate a humble God."[15]

COMMENTARY ON JOHN 6—
THE BREAD OF LIFE

We need the humility of Christ. We need the purity of the heart of Christ. We live by his [eternal] life when we eat his flesh, drink his blood and abide in him.

[On vv. 37–38]: *"All that the Father gives to me will come to me: and whoever comes to me I will never cast out."* What is this being "in" from which there is no being "cast out"? A great inner sanctum, a sweet secret place! A secret place that knows no tediousness. A place without the bitterness of evil thoughts. A place without the intrusion of temptation and grief. Is not this the secret place into which he will enter to whom God will say: *"Well done, my good and faithful servant, enter into the joy of your Lord!"* (Mt. 25)

"And he who comes to me I will not cast out; because I have come down from heaven not to do my own will but the will of him who sent me." For this reason *"I will not cast out the one who comes to me because I have come down from heaven not to do my own will but the will of the one who sent me."* This is a great mystery when he says: *"He who comes to me I will not cast out."* He adds the reason why he will not cast out the one who comes to him, namely the one who believes in him:….*"Because I have not come to do my own will but the will of the one who sent me."* Who is the one who is thrown out from this sweet and pleasant secret place into which it is stated that the servant who does the will of his master will enter? No one except the proud man. [No one except] the soul that trusts in himself and

seeks his own power. [No one except] the soul that does not have the attitude expressed by the prophet when he says: *"Is not my soul subject to the Lord?"* (Ps. 61) But the soul who, through humility, is subject to the grace of God is never cast out but enters into the joy of the Lord. And so that the cause of all our diseases, namely pride, might be healed, the Son of God came down and became humble.

Why, Man, are you proud? God on your behalf has become humble. You would perhaps be ashamed to imitate a humble man, at least imitate a humble God. The Son of God came as a man and became humble. He gives you the precept to be humble. He does not order you to change from being a man and to become a beast. This God became a man; you, O Man, recognize that you are a man. The whole of your humility consists in this that you recognize who you are. And so since God is teaching humility he said: *"I did not come to do my own will but the will of the one who sent me."* This is the way he commends humility. Pride indeed does its own will, humility does the will of God. Therefore *"he who comes to me I will not cast out."* Why? *"Because I have not come to do my own will but the will of the one who sent me."* He came humbly, he came to teach humility. The master of humility came. *"He who comes to me, becomes one body with me: he who comes to me, becomes humble. He who clings to me, will be humble, because he will not do his own will but God's will; and therefore he will not be cast out"*; because when Adam became proud he was cast out (Gn. 3): but Christ when he was humbled was *"raised high above every name whether in heaven or on earth."* (Eph. 1) He, the teacher of humility, came not to do his own will but the will of the one who sent him. Let us come to him, let us come inside him, let us become one body with him so that we may not do our own will but the will of God; and that he may not cast us out because we are parts of his own body because he wanted to be our head by teaching us humility. To him no one can come unless he is humble, from him no one is cast out unless he is proud....

[On vv. 56–58]: Now finally he explains how what he spoke of happens and what it is to eat his body and drink his blood. *"And he who eats my body and drinks my blood remains in me and I remain*

in him." So this is what it means to eat this food and drink this cup—to remain in Christ and to have him remain in us. And for this reason a person who does not remain in Christ and in whom Christ does not remain without a doubt fails to eat this flesh in a spiritual way even though he bites with his teeth in a visible physical way the sacrament of the body and blood of Christ; but rather such a person eats and drinks the sacrament of so great a reality to his own judgment because in an unclean state he presumes to come to Christ's sacrament which a person may not worthily receive unless he is clean: of [those who remain in Christ] it is said: *"Happy are the clean of heart for they shall see God."* (Mt. 5)

"Just as the living Father sent me," he said, *"and I live because of the Father, so he who eats me will live because of me."*

The Son does not become better by his sharing in the Father for he has this sharing by nature. But we are made better by our sharing in the Son through our union with his body and blood which is brought about by this eating and drinking. For we live because of him when we eat him in that we receive from him that eternal life which we do not have in our own right. But he lives because of the Father since he was sent by the Father when he emptied himself and became obedient even to the wood of the Cross.

"Just as the living Father sent me and I live because of the Father, so he who eats me will live because of me." He seems to be saying: I live because of the Father; that is to say I refer my life to him as to one greater than I because my emptying myself has made it so; it is in this emptying that he has sent me. However it is in eating me that a person shares my life and lives because of me. So, just as I, in my humbled state, live because of my Father, such a one raised up lives because of me. He did not speak of that nature in which he is always equal to the Father but of that through which he became less than his Father. He had said earlier on: *"As the Father has life in himself so he has given the Son life in himself."* That is, he has begotten a Son who has life in himself. *"This is the bread that came down from heaven"* that, by eating it, we might have life, who of ourselves cannot have eternal life.

NINTH CENTURY

ST. PASCHASIUS RADBERTUS
ST. ODO OF CLUNY

lifting the blind bread

lifting the blind bread
above the wine-dark cup

"…through Him
with Him
in Him
in the unity
of the Holy Spirit…"

all that seems to be
no longer is
except the pain, darkness
and separation
in the nocturnal waiting

St. Paschasius Radbertus

Paschasius Radbertus was born in Soissons, France, about the year 786. He entered the Benedictine monastery at Corbie, was elected abbot in 843, but resigned in 849 to devote himself entirely to writing. In his work "On the Body and Blood of the Lord," he strongly affirms the real presence of Christ, "the flesh born of Mary," but insists on the "spiritual" mode of this presence. He was attacked by Ratramnus, a contemporary of his at Corbie, who used the term figurative to describe the real presence of Christ in the Sacrament. Ratramnus's position was later condemned as incompatible with the change that is believed to take place at the consecration.[16] Radbertus died around 860.

ON THE BODY AND BLOOD OF THE LORD

Christ immolated "mystically" each day for the life of the world

No one who believes the divine words will doubt that this sacrament becomes in truth the Body and Blood by the Consecration of the Mystery. For Truth says, "My Flesh is true food and my Blood is true drink" (Jn.5:55)…Therefore if it is truly food it is also true Flesh, and if it truly is drink, it is also true Blood…

But because it is not right that Christ [himself] be devoured by teeth, he willed that this bread and wine be truly and efficaciously created his Flesh and Blood in Mystery by the Consecration of the Holy Spirit, who creates it to be immolated mystically and daily for the life of the world, so that, just as true Flesh was created from the Virgin by the Holy Spirit and without intercourse, so the same Body and Blood of Christ might be mystically consecrated from the substance of bread and wine by the same Spirit.

St. Odo of Cluny

St. Odo was born at Tours in 879 and brought up in the family of William of Aquitaine. He studied in Paris, returned to Tours, read the Rule of St. Benedict, and was admitted by Abbot Berno to the monastery at Baume. After the foundation of Cluny, Berno put Odo in charge of the monastery school at Baume. In 927 he succeeded Berno at Cluny. During his abbacy,

he planted the seeds for the monastery's influence in the next two cen-
turies. Odo wrote moral essays and the hymn to the Holy Eucharist, an
English version of which is published here.[17] *He died in 942.*

THE SACRAMENT OF THE BODY AND BLOOD OF THE LORD

God teaches that his servants who
have come to heaven's feast
are pure and so their serving Lord
need only wash their feet.

From many gifts he chose one food,
the grain and grape he called,
one loaf, one cup were chosen out
to be the food of all.

A modest loaf of small expense
and very easily baked,
a little bread enough for all
he takes and consecrates.

Yet this same bread was so sublime
that it could hold within
the whole of God, who now had come
to purge the world of sin.

And it was fitting that one loaf
made from so many grains
should be one body for the Head
that unifies the limbs.

This shining, hidden, simple bread,
this blaze of light divine,
will fill us with his godhead now
and till the end of time.

Tenth Century

St. Symeon the New Theologian

~~~

Unless a Grain

I am still stunned
at being
a grain
of wheat

dropping
in slow motion
into
the earth
at times almost leaping
but always longing
to watch and not be the explosion!

St. Symeon the New Theologian

Born in 949, St. Symeon entered the imperial service in Constantinople as a youth. In 977 he embraced monastic life at Stoudion. Told to leave because of his "extremism," he joined the monastery St. Mamas, where he was elected abbot after only three years. The Discourses contain his instructions to his monks on penance and reform. His theology was sound on the central doctrines: the Trinity, the Incarnation, the divinization of man through grace, and the importance of the sacraments—especially baptism, what was then called penance, and the Eucharist. But his erroneous teaching that monks who are not priests have the power to absolve sins led to his being exiled to the Bosphorus. He died there in 1022.[18]

DISCOURSE 10

Communion with his Body and Blood gives us life and restores us to holiness and sinlessness—it gives us true freedom.

But God came down and was incarnate and became man like us, "but without sin" (Heb 4:15) and destroyed sin....He destroyed altogether the curse of Adam. He died, and by His own death He destroyed death. He rose, and did away with the power and activities of the enemy who had held sway over us through death and sin. As He applied the ineffable and life-giving power of His Godhead and His flesh to the deadly venom and poison of sin, He completely delivered all our race from the action of the enemy. Through Holy Baptism and the Communion of His undefiled Mysteries, His Body and His precious Blood, He cleanses us and gives us life and restores us to holiness and sinlessness. More than that, He sends us forth to enjoy the honor of liberty, so that we may not appear to serve our Master by compulsion, but out of free choice. In the beginning Adam was free and without sin and violence; yet of his own free will he obeyed the enemy and was deceived by him and transgressed God's commandment. So we have been born again in Holy Baptism and have been released from slavery and become free, so that the enemy cannot take any action against us unless we of our own [free] will obey him.

ELEVENTH CENTURY

ST. ANSELM

Learn From Me

the grain pounded
to powder
mixed with water
rolled and baked
to become
ordinary bread

the grapes harvested
trodden
strained
and kept to become
in time
ordinary wine

the Tree of Agony
the Empty Tomb
breakfast on the shore
"If you love me,
Simon Peter,
feed my lambs."

intimacy with God
no ordinary food

ST. ANSELM

Anselm was born in Aosta, Italy, in 1033. He was attracted to Lanfranc's reputation as a great teacher and joined the abbey of Bec in Normandy around the year 1060. Anselm's prayers and meditations date from this period. In 1077, he wrote his Proslogion, *which includes the famous "ontological argument" for the existence of God that still fascinates philosophers. He succeeded Herluin as abbot of Bec, and, when Lanfranc died, Anselm succeeded him and was elected archbishop of Canterbury. King William II was against it, and controversy broke out over the pope's right to appoint bishops. Under Henry I, an agreement was hammered out with Pope Paschal. Anselm died in Canterbury in 1109.*[19]

PRAYER BEFORE RECEIVING THE BODY AND BLOOD OF CHRIST

Lord Jesus Christ,
by the Father's plan and by the working of the Holy Ghost
of your own free will you died
and mercifully redeemed the world
from sin and everlasting death.
I adore and venerate you
as much as ever I can,
though my love is so cold, my devotion so poor.
Thank you for the good gift
of this your holy Body and Blood,
which I desire to receive, as cleansing from sin,
and for a defense against it.

Lord, I acknowledge that I am far from worthy
to approach and touch this sacrament;
but I trust in that mercy
which caused you to lay down your life for sinners
that they might be justified,
and because you gave yourself
willingly as a holy sacrifice to the Father.
A sinner, I presume to receive these gifts
so that I may be justified by them.

I beg and pray you, therefore, merciful lover of men,
let not that which you have given for the cleansing of sins
be unto me the increase of sin,
but rather for forgiveness and protection.

Make me, O Lord,
so to perceive with lips and heart
and know by faith and by love,
that by virtue of this sacrament I may deserve to be
planted in the likeness of your death and resurrection,
by mortifying the old man,
and by renewal of the life of righteousness.
May I be worthy to be incorporated into your body
"which is the church,"
so that I may be your member and you may be my head,
and that I may remain in you and you in me.
Then at the Resurrection you will refashion
the body of my humiliation
according to the body of your glory,
as you promised by your apostle,
and I shall rejoice in you for ever
to your glory,
who with the Father and the Holy Spirit
live and reign for ever. Amen

TWELFTH CENTURY

ST. HILDEGARD OF BINGEN
ST. FRANCIS OF ASSISI

Your Death Was Ugly as the Cry of Steel

Your death was ugly as the cry of steel
cold and lonely
into the noon night

the terror and the horror
of the nailing
steel on steel on steel on steel on steel

the unmitigated wall
of pain—a barrier that loomed
like an arch across the sky
with all, all, empty of sense

and against the groans and shrieks of agony
from savaged nerves
one word emerged

forgive

St. Hildegard of Bingen

Hildegard was born in 1098 of a noble family in Bermersheim. At the age of eight she was entrusted to Bl. Jutta, a recluse attached to the Benedictine monastery of Disibodenberg. When Jutta died, Hildegard became abbess. As a young woman she had already experienced visions and, in 1141, at the request of her confessor, she began to commit them to writing. Scivias *was the result. Her reputation for holiness and wisdom spread, and emperors, prelates, and priests were among her correspondents. Around 1152 she moved her community to Rupertsberg near Bingen. Besides* Scivias, *she wrote hymns, reflections on nature, medical texts, and musical plays, including Ordo Virtutum. She died in 1179.*[20]

LETTER 43

Advice to an Anonymous Priest who has written to St. Hildegard with questions about the Eucharist

[The priest's letter:] Gaius, a humble priest from the companions of Christ, turns to Hildegard, that chaste dove hiding in the clefts of the rock, for help for his eternal salvation, for he sees the intimate and devout nature of her prayer life.

Because, through God's grace your salutary light shines before men, I give glory to your Father who has set you up as a blazing torch to bring light to the Church. Frail sinner though I am, I am filled with joy at seeing your sanctity through which, in a marvelous and unique way, you cling to the embrace of your heavenly Spouse. How could I forget that charity of yours! Day and night I desire to be in your presence and to see your face and, when your body is absent, at least to attempt to grasp you with my mind. So I ask you if you would commend in your perfection to the Spouse, in whose shade you recline, this beggar beside the road that I am, so that the passing crowd may not silence my cries but that, led to the Lord by your prayers, I may receive healing and enlightenment in my blindness.

So enlighten me about the Body and Blood of Christ, the source of all hope for the faithful.

Since the Lord in all matters pours into you wisdom about the things that are fitting for the glory of his Holy Church, clarify for me, as a priest, what is the correct way and the incorrect way to approach this very sacrament.

[Hildegard's answer:] In a true vision with my eyes wide open I heard these words about the sacrament of the Lord's Body and I saw the following:

God remained what He was and He took on what he was not.

That is to say: The Divinity remained for all eternity what it has been from the beginning of time as totally indivisible.

But the incarnation of the Son, which reposed from before time predestined in the heart of the Father, did not yet appear as flesh and blood.

But, at the time when it was predestined to happen, the Son put on flesh—through the strength of his courage he girded himself with flesh as it is written: "The Lord girded himself with power."

And the angel brought the message of his clothing himself in the holy incarnation to a simple virgin in whom he found the basic humility that God had put there. This was seen when, at the words "The Holy Spirit will come upon you and the power of the Most High will overshadow you," she replied [by] calling herself the handmaid of the Lord. The Holy Spirit visited her in a way that goes beyond all human knowledge, pouring himself into her in a way different from any that had previously occurred when a woman conceived. Therefore the same power of the Most High which produced the flesh in the womb of the virgin causes, at the words of the priest, the bread and wine offered on the altar to be changed into the sacrament of his Body and Blood. This happens in such a way that the birth, the passion, the burial, the resurrection and the ascension of the Son of the most high Father appears in this same sacrament as the circle of a coin reveals its Lord. And this happens so that the wounds of men, who are always sinners, always involved as they are in the sin brought through Adam's transgression, may be cleansed and anointed and healed by the blood from the wounds of Christ and so might become his limbs and remain so until the last day....

And I also saw the following:

Even if the priest, on account of the huge number of the suppurating wounds of his sins, lacks the dignity of holiness—as long as he has not been bound by interdict by his Superiors—still the power of the Most High works his miracles in this same oblation. So all who receive faithfully that same sacrament from his hand are filled with light as from the rays of the sun.

If the priest is a righteous man, in faith and in deed, his own soul shines out above the brilliant radiance of the sun. But all those who, by the counsel of the ancient serpent, foster illusions and schisms in this most holy offering, are like the lost angels who denied that God alone was to be honored since they wanted to be like him. And similarly these men want to satisfy their own particular desires through these sacraments. For this reason they will perish along with the lost angels unless they run back to God through the confession of their sins, undertaking penance and crying out with tears: "Woe is me! Woe is me! for I have sinned!"

If they do this God the Father will accept them back for they unknowingly have wounded his own Son.

St. Francis of Assisi

Francis was born in Assisi in 1181, son of Bernardone, a cloth merchant. High-spirited and fun-loving, he became a soldier at twenty-one. A voice called him home from campaigning. One day during Mass, he heard the Gospel: "Go sell all you have, give it to the poor; come, follow me." He did so. When twelve men had joined him, he wrote a rule: in poverty they were to be itinerant beggars preaching the Gospel. The order grew, and Innocent III approved it. Francis then tried to evangelize the Muslims— unsuccessfully. Two years before he died, he received the stigmata. His charism: "Live the Gospel. Preach the Gospel, whether with silence or with words."[21] He died in 1226.

LETTER TO THE GENERAL CHAPTER

We must give ourselves totally to God who, in this amazing way, is present on the altar.

Remember your dignity, then, my friar-priests. *You shall make and keep yourselves holy,* because God is holy. (Lev. 11:44) In this mystery God has honored you above all other human beings, and so you must love, revere and honor him more than all others. Surely this is a great pity, a pitiable weakness, to have him present with you like this and be distracted by anything else in the whole world. Our whole being should be seized with fear, the whole world should tremble and heaven rejoice, when Christ the Son of the living God is present on the altar in the hands of the priest. What wonderful majesty! What stupendous condescension! O sublime humility! O humble sublimity! That the Lord of the whole universe, God and the Son of God, should humble himself like this and hide under the form of a little bread, for our salvation. Look at God's condescension, my brothers, and *pour out your hearts before him (Ps. 61:9).* Humble yourselves that you may be exalted by him. Keep nothing for yourselves, so that he who has given himself wholly to you may receive you wholly.

Thirteenth Century

St. Bonaventure
St. Thomas Aquinas
St. Gertrude

Adoro te devote latens deitas

O how I adore you, deeply hidden God,
Here beyond my senses truly you lie hid;
All my heart I give you, all my mind as well,
Gazing now upon you all my senses fail.

Sight and touch and taste seem here to be obtuse,
Only hearing serves me: words—but where is proof?
I believe the words once spoken by God's Son—
If the Truth spoke falsely, would not truth be gone?

Calvary extinguished all his godhead claims,
Here his total manhood seems an empty name.
Still I trust completely both are here through grace
And I ask for mercy like the dying thief.

Thomas touched your wounds and saw the trace of blood.
I did not, but claim you as my Lord and God.
May I always trust you with a hope so deep
That my love may deepen even as I seek.

Bread of Life, reminder of our Savior's death,
You give us a new life, your immortal breath,
Grant that I may know you, light within my mind,
And may always savor your own life in mine.

Pelicans may suckle with their very blood,
You, O Lord, have fed us with yourself as food.
By your blood O cleanse me, save me through your pain;
Every single drop can save the world from sin.

Jesus, whom I now see veiled before my eyes,
Grant what I so long for even as you hide,
That one day in glory happy through God's grace,
I at last may see you radiant face to face.

St. Bonaventure

Called John when he was born in 1221 in Viterbo, Italy, Bonaventure took the name he is known by when he became a Franciscan. He studied in Paris and became a doctor of theology. In 1257 he was elected minister general of the order. Gentle, courteous, and compassionate, he brought moderation to the faction-torn order by allowing an interpretation of Francis's "poverty" that permitted studying and teaching in universities. Bonaventure wrote The Life of Francis, *the official biography requested by the Franciscan Order. He taught that all human wisdom was folly compared to the mystical light God gives to the faithful Christian. The pope made Bonaventure bishop of Albano, so he attended the Second Council of Lyons. He died in 1274 before the council had concluded.*[22]

THE TREE OF LIFE

A description of Jesus' actions at the Last Supper

16. Among all the memorable events of Christ's life, the most worthy of remembrance is that last banquet, the most sacred supper. Here not only the paschal lamb was presented to be eaten but also the immaculate Lamb, *who takes away the sins of the world* (John 1:29). Under the appearance of bread *having all delight and pleasantness of every taste* (Wisdom 16:20), he was given as food. In this banquet the marvelous sweetness of Christ's goodness shone forth when he dined at the same table and on the same plates with those poor disciples and the traitor Judas. The marvelous example of his humility shone forth when, girt with a towel, the King of Glory diligently washed the feet of the fishermen and even of his betrayer. The marvelous richness of his generosity was manifest when he gave to those first priests, and as a consequence to the whole church and the world, his most sacred body and his true blood as food and drink so that what was soon to be a sacrifice pleasing to God and the priceless price of our redemption would be our viaticum, and sustenance. Finally the marvelous outpouring of his love shone forth when, *loving his own to the end* (John 13:1), he strengthened them in goodness with a gentle exhortation, especially forewarning Peter to be firm in faith and offering to John his breast as a pleasant and sacred place of rest.

O how marvelous are all these things,
how full of sweetness,
but only for that soul
who, having been called to so distinguished a banquet,
runs
with all the ardor of spirit
so that he may cry out
with the Prophet:
As the stag longs for the springs of water
so my soul longs for you,
O God!

St. Thomas Aquinas

Thomas Aquinas was born of an aristocratic Neapolitan family in 1225. He was placed with the Benedictines at Monte Cassino but eventually, against his family's wishes, joined the Dominicans. He studied in Cologne and later taught in Paris and Italy. He saw how reason related to faith and articulated it. He was a man of prayer—what he once glimpsed in a mystical experience led him to call all his writings straw in comparison. His Summa Contra Gentes *was a bridge to the non-Christian world; his* Summa Theologica, *a synthesis of Catholic belief; his* Office of Corpus Christi *reveals a poet as well as a philosopher, as his sermon on the subject demonstrates. Aquinas died in 1274 at the age of forty-nine and is considered perhaps the greatest Catholic theologian.*[23]

SERMON FOR THE FEAST OF CORPUS CHRISTI

Jesus, wanting us to share in his divinity, assumed our nature. Nothing could be more wonderful than this sacrament.

The only-begotten son of God, wishing to enable us to share in his divinity, assumed our nature, so that becoming man he might make men gods.

Moreover, he turned the whole of our nature, which he assumed, to our salvation. For he offered his body to God the Father on the altar of the cross as a sacrifice for our reconciliation; and he shed his blood for our ransom and our cleansing, so that we might be redeemed from wretched captivity and cleansed from all sins.

Now in order that we might always keep the memory of this great act of love, he left his body as food and his blood as drink, to be received by the faithful under the appearances of bread and wine.

How precious and wonderful is this banquet, which brings us salvation and is full of all delight! What could be more precious? It is not the meat of calves or kids that is offered, as happened under the old law; at this meal Christ, the true God, is set before us for us to eat. What could be more wonderful than this sacrament?

No sacrament contributes more to our salvation than this; for it purges away our sins, increases our virtues, and nourishes our minds with an abundance of all the spiritual gifts.

It is offered in the Church for the living and the dead, so that it may be beneficial to all, as it was instituted for the salvation of all.

Finally, no one is capable of expressing the delight of this sacrament, through which the sweetness of the Spirit is tasted at its source, and the memory is celebrated of that surpassing love which Christ showed in his passion.

And so, in order to imprint the immensity of this love more deeply in the hearts of the faithful, at the Last Supper, when the Lord had celebrated the pasch with his disciples and was about to pass from this world to his Father, he instituted this sacrament as a perpetual memorial of his passion. It fulfilled the types of the Old Law; it was the greatest of the miracles he worked; and he left it as a unique consolation to those who were desolate at his departure.

St. Gertrude

Born in 1256, St. Gertrude was placed at age five in Helfta, a Cistercian-inspired convent in Thuringia. Educated there, she underwent a profound conversion experience at the age of twenty-five. From that moment on, her prayer life took on a new intensity. She started having visions during the Divine Office. Through these visions she came to experience Jesus in his humanity, which developed in her a spirituality akin to what later became devotion to the Sacred Heart. Besides the accounts of her visions,

Exercitia spiritualia, *some of which were put together from her notes, she also wrote prayers. She is regarded as one of the most important of the mediaeval mystics.*[24] *She died in 1302.*

A VISION OF JESUS

Christ's love for each person even in their imperfect and unprepared state of soul

Once, when Gertrude heard the bell which called her to Communion, and the chant had already commenced, as she felt that she was not sufficiently prepared, she said to Our Lord: "Behold, Lord, Thou art coming to me; but why hast Thou not granted me the grace of devotion, so that I might present myself before Thee with a better preparation?" He replied: "A bridegroom admires the personal beauty of his bride more than her ornaments; and in like manner I prefer the virtue of humility to the grace of devotion."

Once, when many of the religious had abstained from Communion, Gertrude returned thanks to God, saying, "I thank Thee, O Lord, that Thou hast invited me to Thy sacred Banquet." To which Our Lord replied, with words full of sweetness and tenderness: "Know that I have desired thee with My whole heart." "Alas, Lord!" she exclaimed, "what glory can accrue to Thy divinity when I touch this Sacrament with my unworthy lips?" He replied: "Even as the love which we have for a friend makes us take pleasure in hearing him speak, so also the charity which I have for My elect makes Me sometimes find satisfaction in that in which they find none."

FOURTEENTH CENTURY

JOHN TAULER
ST. NICHOLAS CABASILAS
JULIAN OF NORWICH
ST. CATHERINE OF SIENA

Weave a Song within the Silence

Weave a song within the silence
That these mysteries create
Of the Body of the Savior
Who was tortured for our sake
And the Blood that left his body
Saving sinners from their fate.

Mary bore him, sinless Virgin,
When to this our world he came
To walk freely through the furrows
Scattering his Father's grain
Till he ended his brief visit
With a harvest reaped in pain.

While reclining that last evening
Taking supper with his friends,
When the paschal meal was ended
With the rites the law demands,
He gave them as bread his body,
Broken in his sacred hands.

See the wonder of this moment!
Watch with awe what comes to be!
He, the Word made flesh, has spoken
And the bread and wine perceived
Are now truly his own body
Feeding all who will believe.

Humbly we bow down before him
And in awe we do proclaim
This his presence on our altar
Glorified beyond all pain.
What our senses cannot master
By our faith we now acclaim.

Honor, praise and thanks be given
To the Father and the Son.
Sing with joy in their own Spirit
Who alone can make us one,
And from heaven now with power
Gently to our hearts has come.

JOHN TAULER

John Tauler was born in Strasbourg in 1300. He joined the Dominicans in 1315 and studied in Cologne where Meister Eckhardt was teaching. Tauler developed a great reputation as a preacher and a director of nuns. He wrote no theological works but his sermons, which reveal the depth of his prayer life, were copied down by his brethren and later published. In his life he seems to have achieved a happy blend of the contemplative and the active. This was particularly evident in his service of those hit by the plague in 1348. He died in Strasbourg in 1361.[25]

THE FOOD OF LOVE

The mystery of our union with God effected by the Eucharist, a union more intimate than the human mind can conceive

It is impossible for us to describe in words the ineffable dignity of the soul, and we cannot in any way comprehend it. If we had here with us a human being in his primal nobility, pure as Adam in paradise, in his natural state apart from grace, his simple nature unadorned — that person would be so luminous and pure, so ravishing and richly favored by God that no one would be able to comprehend his purity, nor with his reason conceive of it. How then can reason possibly grasp that immensity beyond all being where the precious food of the Eucharist is, in some marvelous way, made one with us, drawing us wholly to itself and changing us into itself? It is a union more intimate than any that the human mind can conceive, totally unlike any other change; a union more complete than that of a tiny drop of water losing itself in the wine-vat and becoming one with the wine, or that of the rays of the sun made one with the sun's splendor; or the soul with the body, the two together making but one person, one being. In this union the soul is lifted above the infirmity of its natural state, its own insufficiency, and there it is purified, transfigured, and raised above its own powers, its human operations, and its very self. Both being and activities are penetrated through and through by God; formed and transformed interiorly in a divine manner, the soul's new birth is accomplished in truth, and the spirit, losing all its native incompatibility, flows into divine union....

This food of love draws the soul above distinction or difference, beyond resemblance, to divine unity. This is what happens to the transfigured spirit. When the divine heat of love has drawn out all moisture, heaviness, unfitness, then this holy food plunges such a one into the life of God. As our Lord himself said to Saint Augustine: "I am the food of the strong; believe and feast on me. You will not change me into yourself; rather you will be changed into me."

St. Nicholas Cabasilas

Nicholas Cabasilas was born in Thessalonica in 1322. As a layman he studied in Constantinople—his Uncle Nilos being one of his teachers. For ten years he served as counselor to Emperor John VI. The latter part of his life was spent in the monastery of Mangana. His work On Life in Christ *describes the spiritual life from the perspective of the Incarnation which is seen as "repeated and continued in the sacraments of the Church." The incarnate Word finds a Godlike kernel in each human being and this "new life" is brought to fulfillment "in Christ." He died in 1395 and was proclaimed a saint by the Greek Orthodox Church in 1983.*[26]

THE SACRAMENTS OF CHRISTIAN INITIATION

We are transformed to God's own level. Through communion, Christ dwells in us. It is now no longer I who live but Christ who lives in me.

Christ is present in each of the sacraments: he himself confirms us and cleanses us, and he is our food. He is present to those receiving the sacraments of initiation, though in different ways. In baptism he takes away the stain of sin and imprints his own image on the baptized. In confirmation he brings into action the gifts of the Holy Spirit, of which his own flesh is the repository. But when he leads communicants to his table and gives them his body to eat he completely transforms them, raising them to his own level. This is the last sacrament we receive because it is impossible to go beyond it or to add to it anything whatever.

We remain imperfect even after baptism has produced in us its full effect because we have not yet received the gifts of the Holy

Spirit, which are given in confirmation. Those baptized by Philip did not receive the Holy Spirit simply by the grace of baptism: it was necessary for John and Peter to lay hands on them. As scripture says, *the Holy Spirit had not yet come down on any of them; they had only been baptized in the name of the Lord Jesus. Then Peter and John laid hands on them and they received the Holy Spirit.*

Yet even among those who had been filled with the Spirit and prophesied, spoke in tongues and displayed other such gifts, there were some in the time of the apostles who were so far from being divine and spiritual as to be guilty of envy, rivalry, contention, and other similar vices. This is what Paul referred to when he wrote to them: *You are still unspiritual and are living on a purely human plane.*

They were indeed spiritual by reason of the graces they had received, but these graces did not suffice to free them from all sinfulness.

With the Eucharist, however, it is different. No such charge can be brought against those in whom the bread of life, which has saved them from death, has had its full effect and who have not brought to this feast any wrongful dispositions. If this sacrament is fully effective it is quite impossible for it to allow the slightest imperfection to remain in those who receive it.

If you would know the reason for this, it is because through communion, in fulfillment of his promise, Christ dwells in us and we in him. *He lives in me,* he said, *and I in him.*

When Christ lives in us, what can we lack? When we live in Christ, what more can we desire? He dwells in us and he is our dwelling place. How blessed to have become the dwelling place of such a guest! We at once become spiritual in body and soul and in all our faculties because our soul is united to his soul, our body to his body, our blood to his blood. The consequence is that the higher prevails over the lower, the divine over the human. As Paul says, referring to the resurrection: *What is mortal is swallowed up by life.* And elsewhere he writes: *It is no longer I who live: it is Christ who lives in me.*

JULIAN OF NORWICH

Julian was born around 1342 and died around 1413. By 1373 she was an anchoress (female hermit) in a cell attached to St. Julian's church in Norwich. She received sixteen visions (showings) in which she saw the place of Love in the divine plan. She saw that the passion and resurrection of Jesus are crucial to our understanding of sin and evil: through our sin we come to know the depth of God's merciful love. "Wouldst thou know thy Lord's meaning?...Know it well. Love was his meaning. And I saw full surely in this and in all that before God made us, he loved us."[27]

REVELATIONS OF DIVINE LOVE, CHAPTER 60

Christ as our "mother" feeds us with his own body and blood.

The mother's service is nearest, readiest and surest; nearest: for it is most of kind; readiest: for it is most of love; surest: for it is most of truth. This office no one might nor could ever do to the full, except he alone. We know that our mothers bear us to pain and to dying; a strange thing, that! But our true Mother Jesus, he alone beareth us to joy and to endless living; blessed may he be! Thus he sustaineth us within him, in love and travail unto the full time in which he willed to suffer the sharpest throes and most grievous pains that ever were, or ever shall be; and he died at the last. Yet all this might not fully satisfy his marvelous love. And that shewed he in these high overpassing words of love: "If I could suffer more, I would suffer more." He could no more die, but he would not cease working.

Wherefore it behoveth him to feed us; for the very dear love of motherhood hath made him our debtor. The mother can give her child to suck of her milk. But our precious Mother Jesus, he can feed us with himself; and doth, full courteously and tenderly, with the Blessed Sacrament, that is the precious food of true life. And with all the sweet sacraments he sustaineth us full mercifully and graciously. And this was his meaning in those blessed words, where he said: "I it am that Holy Church preacheth to thee and teacheth thee"; that is to say, all the health and the life of the sacraments. "All the power and the grace of my word, all the goodness that is ordained to thee in Holy Church, I it am."

The mother can lay her child tenderly to her breast. But our tender Mother Jesus can lead us, homely, into his blessed breast, by his sweet open side; and shew us there, in part, the Godhead and the joys of heaven, with a ghostly sureness of endless bliss. And that shewed he in the ninth Revelation, giving the same understanding in the sweet words where he saith: "Lo, how I love thee"—looking into his blessed side, rejoicing.

ST. CATHERINE OF SIENA

Daughter of a prosperous dyer, Catherine was born in Siena, Italy, in 1347. At sixteen she became a Dominican tertiary. Instructed by Christ, she left her home to help the poor and the sick and to convert sinners. Her attractive personality, her holiness, and her wisdom led to a growing demand for her mediation in conflicts. In The Dialogo, *written as an exchange between God and herself, Jesus pleads for repentance and reform. Persuaded by her, Pope Gregory XI left Avignon, and returned to Rome but died one year later. Urban VI was elected, but then schism began. Catherine supported Urban tirelessly, but suffered a stroke and died in 1380, aged thirty-three.*[28]

THE DIALOGUE

An account of Catherine's mystical experience of the Trinity during Mass

111. What tastes and sees and touches this sacrament? The soul's sensitivity. How does she see it? With her mind's eye, so long as it has the pupil of holy faith. This eye sees in that whiteness the divine nature joined with the human; wholly God, wholly human; the body, soul, and blood of Christ, his soul united with his body, and his body and soul united with my divine nature, never straying from me. This, if you remember, is what I revealed to you early in your life and that not only to your mind's eye but to your bodily eyes as well, although because of the great light you soon lost your bodily sight and were left with only your spiritual vision.

I revealed this to you when you had set yourself to resist the battle the devil was giving you in this sacrament, to make you grow in love and in the light of most holy faith. You know that you had gone to the church at dawn to hear Mass, and that before that the devil had been tormenting you. You went to stand at the altar of the crucifix, though the priest had come out to Mary's altar. You stood there considering your sinfulness, fearing that you might have offended me while the devil had been troubling you. And you were considering also how great was my charity that I should have made you worthy to hear Mass at all, since you considered yourself unworthy even to enter my temple. When the celebrant reached the consecration you looked up towards him. And at the words of consecration I revealed myself to you. You saw a ray of light coming from my breast, like the ray that comes forth from the sun's circle yet never leaves it. Within this light came a dove, and dove and light were as one and hovered over the host by the power of the words of consecration the celebrant was saying. Your bodily eyes could not endure the light, and only your spiritual vision remained, but there you saw and tasted the depths of the Trinity, wholly God, wholly human, hidden and veiled under that whiteness. Neither the light nor the presence of the Word, whom in spirit you saw in this whiteness, took away the whiteness of the bread. Nor did the one stand in the way of the other. I did not block your sight either of me, God and human, in that bread, or of the bread itself. Neither the whiteness nor the feel nor the taste was taken away from the bread.

I in my kindness showed this to you. It was your mind's eye, with the pupil of holy faith, that had vision in the end. So the spiritual must be the principal vision, because it cannot be deceived. It is with this eye, then, that you must contemplate this sacrament. This hand it is that touches what the eye has seen and known in this sacrament. The hand of love touches through faith, confirming as it were what the soul sees and knows spiritually through faith.

How is this sacrament tasted? With holy desire. The body tastes only the flavor of bread, but the soul tastes me, God and human. So you see, the body senses can be deceived, but not the soul's. In fact, they confirm and clarify the matter for her, for what her mind's eye has seen and known through the pupil of holy faith, she touches with the hand of love. What she has seen she touches in love and faith. And she tastes it with her spiritual sense of holy desire, that is, she tastes the burning, unspeakable charity with which I have made her worthy to receive the tremendous mystery of this sacrament and its grace.

So you see, you must receive this sacrament not only with your bodily senses but with your spiritual sensitivity, by disposing your soul to see and receive and taste this sacrament with affectionate love.

FIFTEENTH CENTURY

THOMAS À KEMPIS

Anima Christi

May the power of holiness blaze in me
as I live by Christ.
May I be saved from the poison of pride
by the body of Christ.
May I be on fire with living joy
through the blood of Christ.
May I be made pure by the water that flows
from the side of Christ.
May I find patience, endurance and peace
in the passion of Christ.

Hear this prayer, O Jesus Savior,
noble and strong.
Shelter me in the shade of your pain
when I go wrong.
Never allow me to leave you in weakness,
torn by pride.
Save me from powers that lead me to doubt,
hate or deride.
Call me when death casts its shadow upon me
and hope burns low
that with your saints I may praise you for ever.
Lord, make it so.

AMEN

Thomas à Kempis

Thomas Hemerken was born of poor parents in 1380 at Kempen in Germany. In 1399 he entered the house of the Canons Regular near Zwolle where his brother was prior. He lived there for the rest of his life. He wrote, preached, and copied manuscripts, and was much sought after for spiritual direction. The Imitation of Christ is his most famous work. Arranged as four books, each with chapters, the Imitation *includes many short, wise sayings, such as: "Never trust yourself to speak unless you love silence…to give orders, unless you know how to obey them" (I:20). Thomas à Kempis also wrote a book entitled* Prayers and Meditations on the Life of Christ. *He died in 1471.*[29]

THE IMITATION OF CHRIST IV:2

God's great goodness and love is shown in this sacrament.

See where love has its source, see how brightly shines this divine abasement! How deep should our thanks be, how sincere our praise, for this your gift. It was indeed a device to heal and profit our souls, when you brought this Sacrament into being; a sweet and joyous banquet indeed, in which you gave yourself to be our food. What wonderful things you do, Lord! How mighty your power is, how unfailing your truth! You gave the word, and everything came into being; so was it with this Sacrament, because it was you who gave command.

How wonderful a thing it is, worthy of man's belief, yet exceeding the grasp of his mind, that you, my Lord and my God, truly God and truly man, are wholly contained beneath the lowly shape of bread and wine; that you are eaten by him who receives you, and yet not consumed. You, the Lord of all things, who stand in need of nothing, have wished to live in our midst by means of this Sacrament. Keep my heart and my body free from stain, so that with a glad and untroubled conscience I may take part more frequently in this mystery of yours; and may I receive to my eternal salvation this Sacrament that you have blessed and devised to be for your particular honor, your everlasting keepsake.

THE IMITATION OF CHRIST IV:3

It is profitable to receive communion frequently.

Lord God, you who give being and life to all souls, how wonderful is the way in which your love stoops to our lowliness! You do not think it below you to come to a poor, unworthy soul and to appease her hunger with the fullness of your Godhead and your manhood alike! Happy the mind, blessed the soul, that deserves reverently to receive you, her Lord and her God, and in receiving you to be filled with spiritual gladness! How great a Lord is he whom she receives, how beloved a guest; how pleasant a companion, how faithful a friend! How beauteous and noble a spouse she embraces, one that surpasses all other loves, one to be loved more than all that tempts our desire.

THE IMITATION OF CHRIST V:13

The devout soul desires union with Christ in the sacrament.

In fact "there is no other people, however great they may be, whose gods have made themselves as close as you, our God, have made yourself close to all your faithful ones" (Dt. 4:7). To these, in fact, you give yourself as saving food—a source of daily comfort and a means of turning one's heart towards heaven. Is there any other people as glorious as the Christian people? Is there under heaven any creature so loved as that devoted soul into which God himself enters to nourish it with his own glorified body?

O ineffable grace! O wonderful condescension! O immeasurable love! O privilege bestowed on men! But what thing shall I give to the Lord in exchange for such a grace, in exchange for such an extraordinary love? I can give nothing more pleasing than the total gift of my whole heart to my God and of my intimate union with him. Then will I exult in the depths of my being, when my soul is perfectly united with God. Then will God himself say to me: "If you want to be with me, I want to be with you." And I will reply to him: "Be gracious enough to stay with me, Lord; it would please me and I would very much like to be with you. This is the whole of my desire that my heart should be united with yours."

SIXTEENTH CENTURY

St. Thomas More
St. Teresa of Avila
St. Francis de Sales

Magnum Mysterium

the mystery
is how we splice
our lives together
with that of Christ

St. Thomas More

Thomas More, son of Judge John More, was born in London in 1478. After four years with the Carthusians, he found that he was not called to that life. He went on to study law at Oxford, marry, and become a brilliant lawyer. He had three daughters and one son by Jane Colt, his first wife. Wise, prayerful, witty—"born for friendship," as someone described him—More was extremely capable. When Wolsey died, Henry VIII made More his chancellor. Henry needed an annulment of his marriage to Catherine, but Thomas was against it—so was the pope. Henry then broke with Rome, annulled his marriage himself, and married Anne Boleyn. More resigned his office. After the Act of Succession was passed, he refused to take the oath. Imprisoned in the Tower for fifteen months, he was tried and condemned. On July 6, 1535, he was beheaded. His last words were: "I die the king's good servant but God's first."[30]

TREATISE ON RECEIVING THE BLESSED BODY OF OUR LORD WORTHILY

Written in the Tower of London, 1535

They receive the blessed body of our Lord both sacramentally and virtually which in due manner and worthily receive the blessed sacrament. When I say worthily I mean not that any man is so good or can be so good that his goodness could make him of very right and reason worthy to receive into his vile earthly body that holy blessed glorious flesh and blood of almighty God himself, with his celestial soul therein, and with the majesty of his eternal godhead. But that he may prepare himself, working with the grace of God, to stand in such a state as the incomparable goodness of God will… vouchsafe to take and accept for worthy, to receive his own inestimable precious body, into the body of so simple a servant.

Such is the wonderful bounty of almighty God that he not only doth vouchsafe but also doth delight to be with men if they prepare to receive him with honest and clean souls, whereof he saith: My delight and pleasures are to be with the sons of men…. But likewise as at the sight or receiving of this excellent memorial of [our Lord's] death…we must with tender compassion, remember and call to mind the bitter pains of his most painful passion. And yet therewithal rejoice and be glad in the consideration of his incomparable kindness, which in his so suffering for us to our inestimable benefit he shewed and declared towards us. So must we be both sore afraid of our own unworthiness and yet therewith be right glad and in great hope of his unmeasurable goodness. Saint Elizabeth, at the visitation, and salutation of our blessed lady, having by revelation the sure inward knowledge that our lady was conceived with our Lord, albeit that she was herself such as else for the diversity between their ages, she well might and would have thought it be convenient and metely, that her young cousin should come to visit her, yet now because she was mother to our Lord, she was sore amarvelled of her visitation and thought her self far unworthy thereto: and therefore said unto her: Whereof is this, that the mother of our lord should come to me? But yet for all the abashment of her own unworthiness she conceived thoroughly such a glad blessed comfort, that her holy child saint John the Baptist hopped in her belly for joy: Whereof she said: As soon as the voice of thy salutation was in myne ears the infant in my womb lept for joy.

Now like as saint Elizabeth, by the spirit of God had those holy affections, both of reverent considering her own unworthiness in the visitation of the mother of god and yet for all that so great inward gladness therewith, let us at this great visitation, in which not the mother of god, as came to saint Elizabeth, but one incomparably more excelling the mother of god, than the mother of god passed S. Elizabeth, doth so vouchsafe to come and visit each of us with his most blessed presence, that he cometh not into our house but into our self, let us I say call for the help of the same holy spirit, that then inspired her: and praye him at this high and holy visitation so to inspire us, that we may both be abashed with the reverent dread of our own unworthiness and yet therewith conceive a joyful consolation and comfort in the consideration of gods inestimable goodness. And that each of us, like as we may well say with great reverent dread and admiration, Whereof is this that my Lord should come unto me? and not only unto me but also into me, so we may with glad heart truly say at the sight of his blessed presence, the child in my belly, that is to wit, the soul in my body leapeth, good lord, for joy.

Now when we have received our lord and have him in our body, let us not then let him alone, and get us forth about other things and look no more unto him, but let all our business be about him. Let us by devout prayer talk to him, by devout meditation talk with him. Let us say with the prophet: I will hear what our lord will speak within me.

St. Teresa of Avila

Of Castilian aristocracy, Teresa was born in 1515 at Avila, Spain. She joined the Carmelites at Incarnation Monastery when she was twenty. Her convent was large and the observance of the Carmelite Rule was casual. After twenty-five years she underwent a second conversion and started having locutions and visions. Despite strong opposition, she started a new, reformed convent, St. Joseph's, living by the original Rule—which included poverty, enclosure, simple habits, sandals, and a vegetarian diet. A wise, no-nonsense type of person, with endless patience and a good sense of humor, Teresa valued intelligence in her postulants. Under obedience, she wrote her autobiography and several books on prayer. These are still classics. She died in 1582 on the way back from her sixteenth foundation.[31]

THE LIFE OF ST. TERESA OF AVILA

Knowledge of the Lord's great love overcomes the fear of receiving Him.

O Wealth of the poor, how wonderfully canst Thou sustain souls, revealing Thy great riches to them gradually and not permitting them to see them all at once! Since the time of that vision I have never seen such great Majesty, hidden in a thing so small as the Host, without marveling at Thy great wisdom. I cannot tell how the Lord gives me courage or strength to approach Him; I only know that it is bestowed on me by Him Who has granted me, and still grants me, such great favors. I could never possibly conceal this or refrain from proclaiming aloud such great marvels. What must be the feelings of a wretch like myself, weighed down with abominations, who has gone through life with so little fear of God, when she finds herself approaching this Lord of such majesty, Whose will it is that my soul shall see Him? How can I open my mouth, which has uttered so many words against this same Lord, to receive that most glorious Body, full of purity and compassion? For the soul, knowing that it has not served Him, is much more grieved and afflicted by the love shining in that face of such great beauty, so kindly and so tender than it is affrighted by the majesty which it sees in Him.

ST. FRANCIS DE SALES

Francis—born in 1567 at Sales in Savoy, the eldest son of a nobleman—was expected to assume a career in the world. Instead he felt a call to the priesthood. After studies at Padua he turned from law and was ordained in Geneva in 1593. He was sent to win back from Calvinism the people of the Chablais district. With patience and gentleness he achieved it. He became bishop of Geneva in 1602. His Introduction to the Devout Life, *his best known work, is a recipe for holiness in the midst of the ordinary. Gentleness was his habit of being, saying, "You catch more flies with a spoonful of honey than a barrel of vinegar."[32] He died in 1622.*

TREATISE ON THE LOVE OF GOD

The Holy Eucharist was instituted so that each person intimately and personally might experience union with the Savior.

This is the union to which the divine shepherd of souls prompted his dear Sulamite [in the Song of Songs]: *Hold me close to thy heart,* he appealed to her, *close as locket or bracelet fits.*

For a signet ring to leave a good impression on wax, it must not only touch the wax but be pressed down hard; that is how God wants us to be united with him—by a union so close, so tight, that we are stamped with his characteristics.

With us, Christ's love is a compelling motive. A wonderful example of perfect union he offers us, heaven knows! He united himself with our human nature from the first, engrafting it on to his, so that to some extent it might share his life. When Adam's sin ruptured that union, God provided a closer, stronger union in the Incarnation, in which our human nature found itself for ever wedded to the personality of the godhead. Then, so that all men individually might be intimately united to his goodness—not merely human nature as such—he instituted the sacrament of the holy eucharist, which each can share and so achieve personal union with the Savior, in reality and by way of food. It is this sacramental union, Theotimus, which impels us towards and promotes that union of soul with God I am now discussing.

SEVENTEENTH CENTURY

ST. VINCENT DE PAUL

My Peace

I give peace
my peace
a deepness and a calm that keeps
the high waves of grief or pain
of growing distance or indifference
from shattering your frail faith

peace I give
my peace
forged each day upon the anvil of
your crucified and yet undying
pride

peace
my peace
the peace that keeps depression from despair
that finds within the darkest woods
moments of sunlight where the leaves
beam slow smoke in the autumn air
keeping the hope that in a while
all that here is only seen
savored shared or understood
when it is past
always will be yours
within my kingdom

St. Vincent de Paul

Vincent de Paul was born into a peasant family in 1581, in Landes, southwest France. He studied theology at Toulouse University and was ordained at nineteen. Captured by pirates, he spent two years as a slave in Tunisia before converting his master and returning to France. In Paris he met Pierre de Bérulle and decided to devote his life to the poor. He was a tireless man of simple piety and profound prayer. As chaplain of the galleys he did much to relieve the lot of prisoners. He founded the Vincentians to train the clergy for rural communities and, with Louise de Marillac, founded the Sisters of Charity, uncloistered sisters serving the poor. Laity, clergy, rich, poor, outcasts, criminals—Vincent de Paul served Christ in each.[33] *He died in 1660.*

ON HOLY COMMUNION

In communion we experience union with God! This is what we are called to bring to the dying.

My daughters, one of the benefits we derive from making a good Communion is that we become one with God. What! a poor Daughter of Charity who, before her communion is merely what she is, that is to say, a thing not worth very much, now becomes one with God! Ah! my daughters, who would be willing to neglect such a boon? Oh! what a grace! what do you think it is, my daughters, but a pledge of eternity? Could we, my dear Sisters, comprehend anything grander? Oh, now, it is impossible for anything greater than that a poor wretched creature is united with God; Oh! may He be for ever blessed!

But my daughters, one of the reasons that has just occurred to me, and one which I regard as one of the most important as far as your vocation is concerned, is that you are destined by God to prepare souls to die well. Do you think, my daughters, that God merely expects you to bring His poor a morsel of bread, a scrap of meat, some soup and medicines? Oh! no, no, no, my daughters, that was not His design when He chose you from all eternity to render Him the services which you render Him in the person of the poor; He expects you to provide for the needs of the soul as well as for those of the body. They are in need of the heavenly manna; they are in need of the Spirit of God, and where will you find it so that you may communicate it to them? In Holy Communion, my daughters. Little and great, big and small, all need it. And hence you should pay special attention to prepare well for the reception of this Divine Spirit which is given in abundance.

EIGHTEENTH CENTURY

ST. ALPHONSUS LIGUORI

The Hands of Christ

God gives a priest
the hands of Christ
to hold the staff
that leads and guides
His people.

God gives a priest
the hands of Christ
to break the bread
of Life to be
His body for His people.

God gives a priest
the hands of Christ
to know the nails of agony
fastened in loneliness to wood
by and for His people.

God gives a priest
the hands of Christ
raised within the shuttered room
to calm to strengthen and to bless
giving what they do not possess
God's peace for all His people.

St. Alphonsus Liguori

Alphonsus Liguori was born near Naples in 1696, the son of a Neapolitan noble. At the age of sixteen he became a lawyer but, eight years later, after losing a serious case, he decided to leave the profession. He joined a preaching order and in 1726 was ordained. In 1732 he founded the Redemptorists, and in 1743 he was elected superior general for life. In 1745 he wrote the first of many devotional and spiritual works. Moral Theology *was the most influential. He taught that a person was free to accept the milder of two equally probable opinions about the morality of particular actions. His sermons were direct and gentle, even while reminding people of the Day of Judgement and inviting them to reconciliation.*[34] *He died in 1787.*

THE PRACTICE OF THE LOVE OF JESUS

Jesus desires to come to us in communion because lovers desire to be one with their beloved.

Could anyone ever have been able to imagine that the Word become flesh would take on the appearance of bread to become our food unless he himself had already done so? St. Augustine asks whether the saying "eat my flesh and drink my blood" is not madness. When Jesus revealed to his disciples his intention of leaving us this sacrament, they were unable to believe it and abandoned him, saying, "How can this man give us his flesh to eat?" and "This saying is hard. Who can accept it?" (Jn. 6:53, 61) The great love of Jesus Christ has conceived and brought about what human beings could not imagine or even believe. What is the food, Savior of the world, which you desired to give us before you died? "This is my body." (1 Cor. 11:24) This is no earthly food, it is I giving myself to you"....

Jesus desires very much to come to us in Holy Communion: "I have eagerly desired to eat this Passover with you" (Lk. 22:15) According to St. Lawrence Justinian, "This is the voice of the most outspoken love." He left himself to us under the appearance of bread so that everyone might be able to receive him. If he had left himself under the appearance of some rare or costly food, the poor would not have been able to receive him. But he left himself under the appearance of bread, which is cheap and is available to everyone, so that people in every land could find him and receive him....

In order to draw us to receive him in Holy Communion, he invites us to "Come, eat of my food, and drink the wine I have mixed!" (Prv. 9:5) and "eat, friends; drink!" meaning the heavenly bread and wine. (Sg. 5:1) He even imposes a commandment on us: "Take it; this is my body." (Mk. 14:22) He encourages us by promising us paradise: "Whoever eats my flesh and drinks my blood has eternal life." (Jn 6:54) "Whoever eats this bread will live for ever." (Jn. 6:58) He goes as far as threatening us with exclusion from paradise should we refuse: "Unless you eat the flesh of the Son of Man and drink his blood, you do not have life within you." (Jn 6:53) All of these invitations, promises and threats are born of his great desire to come to us in this sacrament.

Here is the reason why Jesus desires so much to come in Holy Communion. According to St. Denis, love always aspires and tends towards union, or as St. Thomas puts it, "Lovers desire that the two become one." He means that people who are truly in love want to be as close to one another as though they were a single person. God's great love has so arranged things that he gives himself to us not just in the eternal kingdom, but even here below he allows us to possess him in the greatest intimacy possible, by giving himself to us under the appearance of bread in this sacrament. He is like the lover in the Canticle: "Here he stands behind our wall, gazing through the windows, peering through the lattices" (Sg. 2:9). Even though we cannot see him in the Eucharist, he sees us and is really present there. He is present so that we can possess him, but hidden in order that we might desire him. Until such time as we come to our homeland, Jesus wishes to give himself completely to us and to remain completely united with us.

NINETEENTH CENTURY

St. Philippine Duchesne
St. Thérèse of Lisieux

The Bread of Union

there is no greater gift
that God can give
beyond himself
and this is what he gives
us in
the Bread of Union

there is no food to feed
our fire of hunger
greater than
the kindling
that he
gives us in
the Bread of Union

there is no deeper
darkness no
abyss of God
more empty than
the darkness that
he gives us in
the Bread of Union

there is no silence
more complete
than God's own silence
unuttered, unspoken
and unthought
within
the Bread of Union

there is no sacrifice
no rooftop into
waiting arms
surrender jumping
more all-requiring than
the calvary surrender
that is ours
within
the Bread of Union

and so there is no
resurrected-life-receiving
moment
greater than that
moment when we
receive
all of our Christ, our God
within
the Bread of Union

nor any thanks
more glorious for all of this
that we are made
able to give
than to the Father
we return within
the mystery that is
the Bread of Union

St. Philippine Duchesne

Rose Philippine Duchesne was born in Grenoble in 1769 into a merchant family. She was educated by Visitation sisters but when she wanted to join their community, her father refused his permission. Later she joined the recently founded Religious of the Sacred Heart and was professed in 1804. Her dream of being sent on a mission to America was eventually realized, and in St. Charles, Missouri, she set up a convent and started a school. As an elderly person, she went to catechize the Potawatomi Indians near Kansas City, but language difficulties forced her to return to St. Charles. The Potawatomi called her "Woman who prays always." She died in 1852.[35]

ADORATION OF THE EUCHARIST

Permission is granted to Philippine to watch all night on Holy Thursday. Her night-watch of Adoration and her experience during it occur before she is allowed to go to America.

"This letter will, no doubt, reach you too late; if not, I give permission for night adoration. You may spend the night as you requested" (Mother Barat, March 28, 1806).

With her dearest devotion sanctioned once more, Philippine went directly after supper to her favorite place before the tabernacle....

Impetuous and whole-hearted, courageous and daring, Philippine gave herself to prayer in her own way: her prayer was her very self in action under the inspiration of the Holy Spirit.

Her account of it, written with simple candor to Mother Barat, reveals the activity of a soul immersed in God, carried out of herself by the intensity of love and the yearning to spend herself to the utmost in spreading the Kingdom of Christ.

"What happiness your letter gave me and how much good it did my soul! For three weeks my heart had been as hard as a rock, but when I read your words it melted like wax before a fire. My eyes were no longer dry, and my heart experienced a sweet joy that I seemed to taste all night, for your letter came before the night-watch of Holy Thursday.

"O blessed night! For a second time I believed my prayer had been granted. I am convinced of it, my dear Mother, because of the pure joy I feel and the firm confidence I have. Oh, if only I might go [to America] before the year is out! I have almost persuaded myself that I shall. All night long [while at Adoration] I was in the New World, and I traveled in good company. First of all I reverently gathered up all the Precious Blood from the Garden, the Praetorium, and Calvary. Then I took possession of our Lord in the Blessed Sacrament. Holding him close to my heart, I went forth to scatter my treasure everywhere, without fear that it would be exhausted. St. Francis Xavier helped me to make this priceless seed bear fruit, and from his place before the throne of God he prayed that new lands might be opened to the light of truth. St. Francis Regis himself acted as our guide, with many other saints eager for the glory of God. All went well, and no sorrow, not even holy sorrow, could find place in my heart, for it seemed to me that the merits of Jesus were about to be applied in a wholly new manner....

"I have tried to be sorrowful for the remainder of Good Friday, but I cannot rouse that sentiment within me—my hope has risen so high. Kneeling respectfully at your feet I am

Your humble and obedient daughter."

Phil D. Good Friday morning [April 4, 1806]

St. Thérèse of Lisieux

Thérèse Martin was born in Alençon in 1873 to very devout parents— Louis Martin, a watchmaker, and Zélie Martin, owner of her own lace- making business. All four of their daughters became Carmelite nuns in the same convent at Lisieux. Thérèse had to receive special permission to join the monastery at fifteen. Professed in 1890, she was made assistant novice-mistress in 1893. In 1896 she developed tuberculosis, and a year later she died at the age of twenty-four. Thérèse had been ordered to write her autobiography. Its publication after her death spread across the globe—as if all needed to hear her simple message. Her "little way" of doing ordinary things for the glory of God became the proof that even ordinary people could become saints. Devotion to her grew rapidly. She was canonized in 1925, declared patroness of the foreign missions in 1927, and named doctor of the church in 1997.[36]

ACT OF OBLATION TO MERCIFUL LOVE

Thérèse *offers herself as a victim, to be plunged in and entirely consumed by the fire of God's love.*

O My God! Most Blessed Trinity, I desire to *Love* You and make You *Loved,* to work for the glory of Holy Church by saving souls on earth and liberating those suffering in purgatory. I desire to accomplish Your will perfectly and to reach the degree of glory You have prepared for me in Your Kingdom. I desire, in a word, to be a saint, but I feel my helplessness and I beg You, O my God! to be Yourself my *Sanctity*!

Since you loved me so much as to give me Your only Son as my Savior and my Spouse, the infinite treasures of His merits are mine. I offer them to You with gladness, begging You to look upon me only in the Face of Jesus and in His heart burning with *Love.*

I offer You, too, all the merits of the saints (in heaven and on earth), their acts of *Love,* and those of the holy angels. Finally, I offer you, O *Blessed Trinity!* the *Love* and merits of the *Blessed Virgin,* my dear *Mother.* It is to her I abandon my offering, begging her to present it to You. Her Divine Son, my *Beloved* Spouse, told us in the days of His mortal life: *"Whatsoever you ask the Father in my name he will give it to you!"* I am certain, then, that You will grant my desires; I know, O my God! that *the more you want to give, the more You make us desire.* I feel in my heart immense desires and it is with confidence I ask You to come and take possession of my soul. Ah! I cannot receive Holy Communion as often as I desire, but, Lord, are You not *all-powerful*? Remain in me as in a tabernacle and never separate Yourself from Your little victim.

I want to console You for the ingratitude of the wicked, and I beg of You to take away my freedom to displease You. If through weakness I sometimes fall, may Your *Divine Glance* cleanse my soul immediately, consuming all my imperfections like the fire that transforms everything into itself.

Feast of the Most Holy Trinity,
In the year of grace, 1895

TWENTIETH CENTURY

BLESSED CHARLES DE FOUCAULD
BLESSED COLUMBA MARMION
ALFRED DELP, SJ
POPE PIUS XII
VATICAN II
BLESSED TERESA OF CALCUTTA

Pivotal

I stand
and watch
the universe
spin past me
like a carousel
a merry-go-round
with me
at the center
winding the wheel
or keeping the button pressed

all six of us
round the altar
hold the wafer
a little above

our hand
"This is the Lamb of God..."

what kind of God
to let his creatures
hold him thus
while the universe
goes flying by

BLESSED CHARLES DE FOUCAULD

Charles de Foucauld was born in Strasbourg in 1858. As a young man he abandoned his faith and joined the army. While he was with his regiment in Algeria, the faith of the Muslims impressed him deeply. Later, in Paris, he met Abbé Huvelin. De Foucauld was converted and, after a long search, he found his vocation: a priest living as a hermit in the Sahara serving the Muslim tribes. His goal was to start a new order that would imitate Christ while living in the midst of the Muslim community. He died in 1916, assassinated by a young Arab. Although he had already written a Rule, the "Little Brothers of Jesus" came into being only after his death.[37]

JOURNAL ENTRY FROM A RETREAT IN NAZARETH, NOVEMBER 1897

A meditation on Jesus in the Eucharist

[Blessed Charles:] It is wonderful, my Lord, to be alone in my cell and converse there with you in the silence of the night— and you are there as God, and by your grace. But to stay in my cell when I could be before the Blessed Sacrament—why, it would be as though St. Mary Magdalene had left you on your own when you were at Bethany to go and think about you alone in her room! It is a precious and devout thing, O God, to go and kiss the places you made holy during your life on earth—the stones of Gethsemane and Calvary, the ground along the Way of Sorrows, the waves of the sea of Galilee—but to prefer it to your tabernacle would be to desert the Jesus living beside me, to leave him alone, going away alone to venerate the dead stones in places where he is no longer. It would be to leave the room he is in—and with it his divine companionship—to go to kiss the floor of a room he was in, but is in no longer. To leave the tabernacle to go and venerate statues would be to leave the Jesus living at my side to go into another room to greet his portrait.

Is it not true that someone in love feels that he has made perfect use of all the time he spends in the presence of his beloved? Apart from then, is not that time used best that is employed in some other place?

[Jesus speaks:] "Wherever the sacred Host is to be found, there is the living God, there is your Savior, as really as when he was living and talking in Galilee and Judea, as really as he now is in heaven. Never deliberately miss Holy Communion. Communion is more than life, more than all the good things of this world, more than the whole universe: it is God himself, it is I, Jesus. Could you prefer anything to me? Could you, if you love me at all, however little, voluntarily lose the grace I give you in this way? Love me in all the breadth and simplicity of your heart."

LETTER TO A DEDICATED WOMAN WHOSE LIFE WAS ONE OF GREAT SUFFERING, DECEMBER 1904

Perpetual adoration as part of the Rule for the order he hopes to found

The work to which I have long seen I ought to dedicate my life is the building up of two little families, one called the "Little Brothers of the Sacred Heart of Jesus," and the other the "Little Sisters of the Sacred Heart of Jesus," both with the same aim: the glorification of God by the imitation of the hidden life of Jesus, the perpetual adoration of the sacred host and the conversion of unbelievers. They would both take the same form: they would be small, enclosed fraternities with about twenty brothers or sisters, in which, following the rule of St. Augustine and special constitutions (with solemn vows when Holy Church permits), the hidden life of Jesus of Nazareth will be followed as faithfully as possible, and the most Blessed Sacrament, exposed day and night, will be perpetually adored in love, adoration, sacrifice, prayer, manual labor, poverty, abasement, recollection and silence. They will be in the most out-of-the-way parts of non-Christian countries, so that Jesus will be brought to the places where he is least known, and search may be made with him for his most lost and abandoned sheep.

Not knowing any more lost, abandoned, deserted country, none more lacking in workers for the Gospel than the Sahara and Morocco, I have asked and obtained permission to set up a tabernacle on their frontiers, and bring a few brothers together there in adoration of the sacred Victim. I have been living here for several years up till now, alone—mea culpa, mea culpa, mea culpa. Unless the grain of wheat falling to the ground dies, it remains alone; if it dies, it brings forth much fruit. I have not died, so I am alone. Pray for my conversion that, dying, I may bear fruit....

BLESSED COLUMBA MARMION

Columba Marmion was born in Dublin in 1858 and studied at Holy Cross, Clonliffe, and also in Rome. After ordination in 1881, he was professor of philosophy at Holy Cross until, in 1886, he went to Belgium and joined the Benedictine Abbey of Maredsous. In 1899 he was made prior of the abbey of Mont César, and then from 1909 till his death in 1923, he was abbot of Maredsous. His teaching was profoundly christocentric: holiness for the Christian, whether lay or cleric, consists in deep union with Christ who lives within us. His books have become spiritual classics, in particular Christ, the Life of the Soul *and* Union with God. *He was beatified by Pope John Paul in 2000.*[38]

CHRIST, THE LIFE OF THE SOUL

We must surrender ourselves with the Divine Victim in the Eucharist.

If we are to be thus accepted by God, we must make our self-offering one with the oblation that Christ made of himself on the cross and renews on the altar. Our Lord substituted himself for us in his sacrifice; he took the place of us all. That is why the blow that fell on him has morally slain us too: *If one died for all, then all have died.* We shall, however, effectively die with him only by uniting ourselves to his eucharistic sacrifice; and how can we be identified with him in his character as victim? By handing ourselves over, as he did, in unreserved obedience to God's good pleasure.

The victim offered to God must be fully at God's disposal. We must, therefore, live in this basic attitude of giving everything, absolutely everything, to God. Out of love for him we must carry out our acts of renunciation and self-denial, and accept daily sufferings, trials and pain, to such a point that we can say, as Jesus said at the hour of his passion: *I act like this so that the world may realize that I love the Father.* This is what self-offering with Jesus implies. We give God the most acceptable homage he can receive from us when we offer the divine Son to his eternal Father, and when we offer ourselves with *this holy and perfect sacrifice* in the same dispositions that filled the sacred heart of Christ on the cross: an intense love for the Father and for our brothers and sisters, a burning desire for the salvation of all, and a total abandonment to the divine will in all things, especially when it goes against the grain and is hard for us.

We find in this the surest means of transformation into Christ, particularly if we unite ourselves to him in communion, which is the most fruitful way of sharing in the sacrifice of the altar. When Christ finds us thus united with him he immolates us with himself, makes us pleasing to his Father, and transforms us more and more into his own likeness.

ALFRED DELP, SJ

Alfred Delp was born in Mannheim, Germany in 1907, his mother a Catholic, his father a Protestant. He was brought up a Protestant but converted to Catholicism and in 1926 became a Jesuit. He taught at St. Blasien College in the Black Forest. Ordained a priest in 1937, he worked as a pastor in St. George's parish in Munich. While serving there he was involved in helping Jews escape to Switzerland. Fr. Delp was involved with the Jesuits' vocal opposition to the Nazi regime and became part of the Kreisau Circle. After the plot against Hitler failed, Delp was arrested on July 20, 1944, and imprisoned. He was found guilty and executed by the Gestapo on February 2, 1945. His journals from prison reveal his courage and his faith.[39]

PRISON JOURNAL ENTRY, 1944

On sitting before the Host and talking with Jesus about his imprisonment

This year the temptation to make an idyllic myth of Christmas will no doubt be less in evidence than usual. The harsh realities of life have been brought home to us as never before. Many who spend Christmas in dug-outs and shelters that would make the stable at Bethlehem seem cozy by comparison will have little inclination to glamorize the ox and the ass....

To breathe again. To be honest I too long to be able to breathe again, to be relieved of my troubles. How earnestly I prayed the prayer for speedy deliverance in yesterday's Mass. Each day I have to steel myself for the hours of daylight and each night for the hours of darkness. In between I often kneel or sit before my silent Host and talk over with him the circumstances in which I am. Without this constant contact with him I should have despaired long ago.

The question that applies to the whole world applies to me personally and concretely on this feast of the nativity. Is there anything different about celebrating Mass here in this narrow cell where prayers are said and tears are shed and God is known, believed in and called on? At stated hours the key grates in the lock and my wrists are put back into handcuffs; at stated hours they are taken off—that goes on day after day, monotonously, without variation. Where does the breathing again which God makes possible come in? And the waiting and waiting for relief— how long? And to what end?

PRISON JOURNAL ENTRY, JANUARY 6, 1945

The Feast of the Epiphany

Thank God my fetters were so loosely fastened that tonight I could slip them off again. So I could celebrate Mass exactly as on Christmas Eve with my hands quite free. And this is the last night before the final stage and I am taking the Lord with me after all. The new hiding place the Marians have supplied me with is easily disposed of, so God will be with me during the proceedings.

PRISON JOURNAL ENTRY, JANUARY 7, 1945

Fr. Delp was executed in the Plotensee prison less than a month after this entry.

The only opportunity to pass anything on occurs just after exercise—hence just a few more lines....

The warder will soon be here. And tomorrow we are off to the "house of silence" [i.e. the Gestapo headquarters]. I wish my mother the joy of today's gospel and that speedily. She has borne enough of sorrow and sacrifice by now. *In the name of the Lord.* I have not written any farewell letters; my innermost feelings are beyond utterance.

POPE PIUS XII

Born in 1876, Eugenio Pacelli, Pope Pius XII, was educated at the Roman seminary and the Gregorian University. Ordained a priest in 1899 he entered the Papal Secretariat of State in 1901. In 1917 he was apostolic nuncio to Bavaria and took an active part in Benedict XV's peace efforts. Pacelli was elected pope in 1939. His encyclical Mediator Dei *(On the Sacred Liturgy) was a major contribution to the reform of the liturgy. In 1951 he restored the Paschal vigil service and subsequently reformed the entire liturgy of Holy Week. In many ways his work set the stage for the reform of the liturgy mandated by Vatican II and continued by Paul VI, John Paul II, and currently by Benedict XVI.[40] He died in 1958.*

MEDIATOR DEI

Through the Eucharist we choose to accept the grace of union with God won for us on Calvary.

77. This purchase, however, does not immediately have its full effect; since Christ, after redeeming the world at the lavish cost of His own blood, still must come into complete possession of the souls of men. Wherefore, that the redemption and salvation of each person and of future generations unto the end of time may be effectively accomplished, and be acceptable to God, it is necessary that men should individually come into vital contact with the sacrifice of the cross, so that the merits, which flow from it, should be imparted to them. In a certain sense it can be said that on Calvary Christ built a font of purification and salvation which he filled with the blood he shed; but if men do not bathe in it and there wash away the stains of their iniquities, they can never be purified and saved.

78. The cooperation of the faithful is required so that sinners may be individually purified in the blood of the Lamb. For though, speaking generally, Christ reconciled by his painful death the whole human race with the Father, He wished that all should approach and be drawn to his cross, especially by means of the sacraments and the eucharistic sacrifice, to obtain the salutary fruits produced by Him upon it. Through this active and individual participation, the members of the Mystical Body not only become daily more like their divine Head, but the life flowing from the Head is imparted to

the members, so that we can each repeat the words of St. Paul, "With Christ I am nailed to the cross: I live, now not I, but Christ liveth in me."

VATICAN II

The Second Vatican Council was summoned by Pope John XXIII to update the Church for the second part of the twentieth century and beyond. He launched the Council in October 1962 and, after his death, it was reassembled by his successor, Pope Paul VI, in October 1963. The Council was concluded in December 1965, having published some sixteen decrees. Sacrosanctum Concilium (Decree on Sacred Liturgy), *its first published decree, focused on the reform of the Sacred Liturgy—the Mass, the Divine Office, and the sacraments. Some forty years later, the reform of the Mass continues. Pope John Paul II published a new* Missale Romanum *in 2002, and at the time of this writing the focal point of controversy remains the adequacy of the translations from the Latin into the vernacular, especially in anglophonic countries.*[41]

SACROSANCTUM CONCILIUM

Liturgy: Through which the work of our redemption is accomplished

10. Nevertheless the liturgy is the summit toward which the activity of the Church is directed; it is also the fount from which all her power flows. For the goal of apostolic endeavor is that all who are made sons of God by faith and baptism should come together to praise God in the midst of his Church, to take part in the Sacrifice and to eat the Lord's supper....

The renewal in the Eucharist of the covenant between the Lord and man draws the faithful and sets them aflame with Christ's insistent love. From the liturgy, therefore, and especially from the Eucharist, grace is poured forth upon us as from a fountain, and the sanctification of men in Christ and the glorification of God to which all other activities of the church are directed, as towards their end, are achieved with maximum effectiveness.

47. At the Last Supper, on the night when He was betrayed, our Savior instituted the Eucharistic Sacrifice of His Body and

Blood. He did this in order to perpetuate the sacrifice of the Cross throughout the centuries until He should come again, and so to entrust to His beloved spouse, the Church, a memorial of His death and resurrection: a sacrament of love, a sign of unity, a bond of charity, a paschal banquet in which Christ is consumed, the mind is filled with grace, and a pledge of future glory is given us.

48. The Church, therefore, earnestly desires that Christ's faithful, when present at this mystery of faith, should not be there as strangers or silent spectators. On the contrary, through a proper appreciation of the rites and prayers they should participate knowingly, devoutly and actively. They should be instructed by God's word and be refreshed at the table of the Lord's body; they should give thanks to God; by offering the Immaculate Victim, not only through the hands of the priest, but also with him, they should learn to offer themselves too. Through Christ the Mediator, they should be drawn day by day into ever closer union with God and with each other, so that finally God may be all in all.

BLESSED TERESA OF CALCUTTA

Blessed Teresa of Calcutta, Agnes Gonxha Bojaxhin, was born in Skopje, Macedonia, in 1910. In 1928 she joined the Sisters of Loretto and in 1929 she began teaching at St. Mary's in Calcutta, their school for girls. Experiencing a profound call from God to work with the poorest of the poor, she eventually got the permissions necessary and left the convent. Some of her former students joined her and she began her first work—a home for the dying. Her Missionaries of Charity, approved in 1950, became the fastest growing order in the Church. In 1978, she was awarded the Nobel Prize for Peace. She died in 1997. The Missionaries of Charity now have houses in the poor areas of many cities across the world. She was beatified by Pope John Paul II in 2003.[42]

JESUS, THE WORD TO BE SPOKEN

The joy of loving is in the Eucharist.

Where will you get the joy of loving?—in the Eucharist, Holy Communion. Jesus has made himself the bread of life to give us life. Night and day, he is there. If you really want to grow in love, come back to the Eucharist, come back to adoration. In our congregation, we used to have adoration once a week for one hour, and then in 1973, we decided to have adoration one hour every day. We have much work to do. Our homes for the sick and dying destitute are full everywhere. And from the time we started having adoration every day, our love for Jesus became more intimate, our love for each other more understanding, our love for the poor more compassionate, and we have double the number of vocations. God has blessed us with many wonderful vocations.

Twenty-First Century

Francis Xavier Nguyen Cardinal Van Thuan

Pope John Paul II

Pope Benedict XVI

Hoc Est Enim Corpus Meum

Take, all of you
and eat.
This is my Body.

Father, forgive them
they know not
what they do.

John,
this is your mother.

Father,
into your hands
I commend my spirit.

It is accomplished.

Mary!
Rabbuni!

Peace be with you!

one long
sentence of redemption
uttered
drop by drop
stalagmited
in time
etched
into the rock
of history

then
retemporized
at each mass

for the Savior's intimacy
with each beloved

FRANCIS XAVIER NGUYEN CARDINAL VAN THUAN

Francis Xavier Nguyen Van Thuan was born in Hue, Vietnam, in 1928. He was ordained a priest in 1953. He received a doctorate in canon law from Rome in 1959 then returned and became rector of the major seminary in Nha Trang. In 1975 Paul VI named him archbishop of Saigon. He was arrested by the Communists and spent thirteen years in jail, nine of them in solitary confinement. Released in 1991, he was expelled from his country and came to Rome, where he served in the Pontifical Council for Justice and Peace. After his release, he wrote several books, many with the theme and title word of hope, such as the one below. In 2000 he was invited by John Paul II to lead the lenten retreat for the curia. He was made a cardinal in 2001 and died in 2002.[43]

TESTIMONY OF HOPE

The most beautiful Masses of my life

Once more, I return to my own experience. When I was arrested, I had to leave immediately with empty hands. The next day, I was permitted to write to my people in order to ask for the most necessary things: clothes, toothpaste....I wrote, "Please send me a little wine as medicine for my stomachache." The faithful understood right away.

They sent me a small bottle of wine for Mass with a label that read, "medicine for stomachaches." They also sent some hosts, which they hid in a flashlight for protection against the humidity.

The police asked me, "You have stomachaches?"

"Yes."

"Here's some medicine for you."

I will never be able to express my great joy! Every day, with three drops of wine and a drop of water in the palm of my hand, I would celebrate Mass. This was my altar, and this was my cathedral! It was true medicine for soul and body, "Medicine of immortality, remedy so as not to die but to have life always in Jesus," as St. Ignatius of Antioch says.

Each time I celebrated the Mass, I had the opportunity to extend my hands and nail myself to the cross with Jesus, to drink with him the bitter chalice. Each day in reciting the words of consecration, I confirmed with all my heart and soul a new pact, an eternal pact between Jesus and me through his blood mixed with mine. Those were the most beautiful Masses of my life!

POPE JOHN PAUL II

Pope John Paul II was born Karol Wojtyla in 1920, in Wadowice, Poland. His mother died when he was nine. During World War II he worked as an actor in a clandestine group that attempted to keep culture alive during the Nazi occupation. Towards the end of the war, he felt called to the priesthood and became part of the underground seminary in Krakow. Ordained in 1946, he was sent to Rome for a doctorate in theology. In 1958 he was made auxiliary bishop of Krakow at thirty-eight. During Vatican II he worked extensively on the decree The Church in the Modern World. *Elected pope in October 1978, he set about continuing the implementation of the decrees of the Council. In the evening of his papacy, in 2003, he wrote* Ecclesia de Eucharistia *(On the Eucharist and Its Relationship to the Church). This encyclical articulated the excitement that his personal faith in the centrality of the Eucharist was bringing to many young people—especially in his World Youth Day gatherings. A final apostolic letter,* Mane Nobiscum *("Stay with Us, Lord") is a dramatic farewell blessing to his entire flock—his funeral in 2005 showed that no one need feel excluded from this blessing.*[44]

ECCLESIA DE EUCHARISTIA

Contemporizing Calvary

5. ...By the gift of the Holy Spirit at Pentecost the Church was born and set out upon the pathways of the world, yet a decisive moment in her taking shape was certainly the institution of the Eucharist in the Upper Room [The Cenacle]. Her foundation and wellspring is the whole *Triduum paschale*, but this is as it were gathered up, foreshadowed and "concentrated" for ever in the gift of the Eucharist. In this gift Jesus Christ entrusted to his Church the

perennial making present of the paschal mystery. With it he brought about a mysterious "oneness in time" [Italian: *contemporaneità*] between that Triduum and the passage of the centuries.

The thought of this leads us to profound amazement and gratitude. In the paschal event and the Eucharist which makes it present throughout the centuries, there is a truly enormous "capacity," which embraces all of history as the recipient of the grace of the redemption. This amazement should always fill the Church assembled for the celebration of the Eucharist. But in a special way it should fill the minister of the Eucharist. For it is he who, by the authority given him in the sacrament of priestly ordination, effects the consecration. It is he who says with the power coming to him from Christ in the Upper Room: "This is my body, which will be given up for you. This is the cup of my blood, poured out for you...." The priest says these words, or rather *he puts his voice at the disposal of the One who spoke these words in the Upper Room* and who desires that they should be repeated in every generation by all those who in the Church ministerially share in his priesthood.

7. This year, the twenty-fifth of my Pontificate, I wish to involve the whole Church more fully in this Eucharistic reflection, also as a way of thanking the Lord for the gift of the Eucharist and the priesthood: "Gift and Mystery." Consequently, I cannot let this Holy Thursday 2003 pass without halting before the "Eucharistic face" of Christ and pointing out with new force to the Church the centrality of the Eucharist.

From it the Church draws her life. From this "living bread" she draws her nourishment. How could I not feel the need to urge everyone to experience it ever anew?

8. When I think of the Eucharist, and look at my life as a priest, as a Bishop and as the Successor of Peter, I naturally recall the many times and places in which I was able to celebrate it. I remember the parish church of Niegowic, where I had my first pastoral assignment, the collegiate church of Saint Florian in Krakow, Wawel Cathedral, Saint Peter's Basilica and so many basilicas and churches in Rome and throughout the world. I have been able to celebrate Holy Mass in chapels built along mountain paths, on lakeshores and sea coasts; I have celebrated it on altars built in stadiums and in city squares. This varied scenario of celebrations of

the Eucharist has given me a powerful experience of its universal and, so to speak, cosmic character. Yes, cosmic! Because even when it is celebrated on the humble altar of a country church, the Eucharist is always in some way celebrated *on the altar of the world.* It unites heaven and earth. It embraces and permeates all creation. The Son of God became man in order to restore all creation, in one supreme act of praise, to the One who made it from nothing. He, the Eternal High Priest who by the blood of his Cross entered the eternal sanctuary, thus gives back to the Creator and Father all creation redeemed. He does so through the priestly ministry of the Church, to the glory of the Most Holy Trinity. Truly this is the *mysterium fidei* which is accomplished in the Eucharist: the world which came forth from the hands of God the Creator now returns to him redeemed by Christ.

POPE BENEDICT XVI

Benedict XVI, Joseph Ratzinger, was born in Bavaria, Germany, in 1927. He was drafted at sixteen, but his unit was never sent to the front. After the war, his academic career as a lively new theologian saw him professor at Bonn University by 1959 and at Münster by 1963. At Vatican Council II, he was a "theological expert" for Cardinal Frings of Munich. In 1966 he was given a chair in theology at Tübingen. In 1977 Paul VI made him Cardinal Archbishop of Munich, and in 1981 John Paul II brought him to Rome to head the Congregation for the Doctrine of the Faith. Cardinal Ratzinger shared the pope's belief that the Vatican II documents had not always been correctly interpreted. He also shared—and continues to share—the pope's growing conviction that relativism is the current cultural heresy. When John Paul II died, Joseph Cardinal Ratzinger was elected pope on April 19, 2005, becoming Benedict XVI. In August of 2005, he continued the tradition of World Youth Day, which John Paul II had started twenty years earlier, addressing the crowd at Mass.[45] *In December 2005, the new pope wrote his first encyclical— Deus Caritas Est (God Is Love), an analysis of how human love and divine love blend together. After the Synod on the Eucharist in 2005, he wrote the apostolic exhortation Sacramentum Caritatis (The Sacrament of Charity).*[46]

HOMILY AT MASS ON WORLD YOUTH DAY, AUGUST 2005

The Eucharist transforms violence into love, death into life. But it is given to us so that we ourselves will be transformed.

Yesterday evening we came together in the presence of the Sacred Host, in which Jesus becomes for us the bread that sustains and feeds us (cf. *Jn* 6:35), and there we began our inner journey of adoration. In the Eucharist, adoration must become union.

At the celebration of the Eucharist, we find ourselves in the "hour" of Jesus, to use the language of John's Gospel. Through the Eucharist this "hour" of Jesus becomes our own hour, his presence in our midst. Together with the disciples he celebrated the Passover of Israel, the memorial of God's liberating action that led Israel from slavery to freedom. Jesus follows the rites of Israel. He recites over the bread the prayer of praise and blessing.

But then something new happens. He thanks God not only for the great works of the past; he thanks him for his own exaltation, soon to be accomplished through the Cross and Resurrection, and he speaks to the disciples in words that sum up the whole of the Law and the Prophets: "This is my Body, given in sacrifice for you. This cup is the New Covenant in my Blood." He then distributes the bread and the cup, and instructs them to repeat his words and actions of that moment over and over again in his memory.

What is happening? How can Jesus distribute his Body and his Blood?

By making the bread into his Body and the wine into his Blood, he anticipates his death, he accepts it in his heart, and he transforms it into an action of love. What on the outside is simply brutal violence—the Crucifixion—from within becomes an act of total self-giving love. This is the substantial transformation which was accomplished at the Last Supper and was destined to set in motion a series of transformations leading ultimately to the transformation of the world when God will be all in all. (cf. *1 Cor* 15:28)

In their hearts, people always and everywhere have somehow expected a change, a transformation of the world. Here now is the central act of transformation that alone can truly renew the world: violence is transformed into love, and death into life.

This first fundamental transformation of violence into love, of death into life, brings other changes in its wake. Bread and wine become his Body and Blood.

But it must not stop there; on the contrary, the process of transformation must now gather momentum. The Body and Blood of Christ are given to us so that we ourselves will be transformed in our turn. We are to become the Body of Christ, his own Flesh and Blood.

We all eat the one bread, and this means that we ourselves become one. In this way, adoration, as we said earlier, becomes union. God no longer simply stands before us as the One who is totally Other. He is within us, and we are in him. His dynamic enters into us and then seeks to spread outwards to others until it fills the world, so that his love can truly become the dominant measure of the world. Jesus' hour is the hour in which love triumphs. In other words: it is God who has triumphed, because he is Love. Jesus' hour seeks to become our own hour and will indeed become so if we allow ourselves, through the celebration of the Eucharist, to be drawn into that process of transformation that the Lord intends to bring about. The Eucharist must become the center of our lives.

SACRAMENTUM CARITATIS

The Eucharist, Christ giving himself totally to us, is the most perfect act of charity.

"As the living Father sent me, and I live because of the Father, so he who eats me will live because of me." (Jn 6:57)

70. The Lord Jesus, who became for us the food of truth and love, speaks of the gift of his life and assures us that "if any one eats of this bread, he will live for ever" (Jn 6:51). This "eternal life" begins in us even now, thanks to the transformation effected in us by the gift of the Eucharist: "He who eats me will live because of me" (Jn 6:57). These words of Jesus make us realize how the mystery "believed" and "celebrated" contains an innate power making it the principle of new life within us and the form of our Christian existence. By receiving the body and blood of Jesus Christ we

become sharers in the divine life in an ever more adult and conscious way. Here too, we can apply Saint Augustine's words, in his *Confessions,* about the eternal *Logos* as the food of our souls. Stressing the mysterious nature of this food, Augustine imagines the Lord saying to him: "I am the food of grown men; grow, and you shall feed upon me; nor shall you change me, like the food of your flesh, into yourself, but you shall be changed into me." (198) It is not the eucharistic food that is changed into us, but rather we who are mysteriously transformed by it. Christ nourishes us by uniting us to himself; "he draws us into himself." (199)

Here the eucharistic celebration appears in all its power as the source and summit of the Church's life, since it expresses at once both the origin and the fulfillment of the new and definitive worship of God, the *logiké latreía.* (200) Saint Paul's exhortation to the Romans in this regard is a concise description of how the Eucharist makes our whole life a spiritual worship pleasing to God: "I appeal to you therefore, my brothers, by the mercies of God, to present your bodies as a living sacrifice, holy and acceptable to God, which is your spiritual worship." (*Rom* 12:1) In these words the new worship appears as a total self-offering made in communion with the whole Church. The Apostle's insistence on the offering of our bodies emphasizes the concrete human reality of a worship which is anything but disincarnate. The Bishop of Hippo goes on to say that "this is the sacrifice of Christians: that we, though many, are one body in Christ. The Church celebrates this mystery in the sacrament of the altar, as the faithful know, and there she shows them clearly that in what is offered, she herself is offered."(201) Catholic doctrine, in fact, affirms that the Eucharist, as the sacrifice of Christ, is also the sacrifice of the Church, and thus of all the faithful. (202) This insistence on sacrifice—a "making sacred"—expresses all the existential depth implied in the transformation of our human reality as taken up by Christ. (cf. *Phil* 3:12)

The all-encompassing effect of eucharistic worship

71. Christianity's new worship includes and transfigures every aspect of life: "Whether you eat or drink, or whatever you do, do all to the glory of God." (*1 Cor* 10:31) Christians, in all their actions, are called to offer true worship to God. Here the intrinsically

eucharistic nature of Christian life begins to take shape. The Eucharist, since it embraces the concrete, everyday existence of the believer, makes possible, day by day, the progressive transfiguration of all those called by grace to reflect the image of the Son of God. (cf. *Rom* 8:29ff) There is nothing authentically human—our thoughts and affections, our words and deeds—that does not find in the sacrament of the Eucharist the form it needs to be lived to the full. Here we can see the full human import of the radical newness brought by Christ in the Eucharist: the worship of God in our lives cannot be relegated to something private and individual, but tends by its nature to permeate every aspect of our existence. Worship pleasing to God thus becomes a new way of living our whole life, each particular moment of which is lifted up, since it is lived as part of a relationship with Christ and as an offering to God. The glory of God is the living man (cf. *1 Cor* 10:31). And the life of man is the vision of God. (203)

The Eucharist, a mystery to be proclaimed: The Eucharist and mission

84. In my homily at the eucharistic celebration solemnly inaugurating my Petrine ministry, I said that "there is nothing more beautiful than to be surprised by the Gospel, by the encounter with Christ. There is nothing more beautiful than to know him and to speak to others of our friendship with him." (233) These words are all the more significant if we think of the mystery of the Eucharist. The love that we celebrate in the sacrament is not something we can keep to ourselves. By its very nature it demands to be shared with all. What the world needs is God's love; it needs to encounter Christ and to believe in him. The Eucharist is thus the source and summit not only of the Church's life, but also of her mission: "an authentically eucharistic Church is a missionary Church." (234) We too must be able to tell our brothers and sisters with conviction: "That which we have seen and heard we proclaim also to you, so that you may have fellowship with us" (*1 Jn* 1:3). Truly, nothing is more beautiful than to know Christ and to make him known to others. The institution of the Eucharist, for that matter, anticipates the very heart of Jesus" mission: he is the one sent by the Father for the redemption of the world (cf. *Jn* 3:16–17; *Rom* 8:32). At the Last Supper, Jesus entrusts to his disciples the sacrament which makes

present his self-sacrifice for the salvation of us all, in obedience to the Father's will. We cannot approach the eucharistic table without being drawn into the mission which, beginning in the very heart of God, is meant to reach all people. Missionary outreach is thus an essential part of the eucharistic form of the Christian life.

Conclusion

97. Through the intercession of the Blessed Virgin Mary, may the Holy Spirit kindle within us the same ardour experienced by the disciples on the way to Emmaus (cf. *Lk* 24:13–35) and renew our "eucharistic wonder" through the splendor and beauty radiating from the liturgical rite, the efficacious sign of the infinite beauty of the holy mystery of God. Those disciples arose and returned in haste to Jerusalem in order to share their joy with their brothers and sisters in the faith. True joy is found in recognizing that the Lord is still with us, our faithful companion along the way. The Eucharist makes us discover that Christ, risen from the dead, is our contemporary in the mystery of the Church, his body. Of this mystery of love we have become witnesses. Let us encourage one another to walk joyfully, our hearts filled with wonder, towards our encounter with the Holy Eucharist, so that we may experience and proclaim to others the truth of the words with which Jesus took leave of his disciples: "Lo, I am with you always, until the end of the world." (*Mt* 28:20)

Exhortation of Pope Benedict XVI following the Synod on the Eucharist in 2005

Closing

The Highpriestly Prayer

O Father, it is my desire
That those You gave to me
Should be with me that where I am
My friends may also be.
To them I have revealed your love,
Your truth, your life, your way;
And now a word abides in them
Which shall not pass away.

The glory that You gave to me,
To them I now have given;
That so they may be one on earth
As we are one in heaven.
Do not, O Father, take them from
The world your hands have made;
But keep them from the Evil one,
From all that is depraved.

And teach them how to give their lives
That new life may abound.
In giving all they find our love
And in that love are found.
O Father, it is my desire
That all may live as one,
With You in me and I in them
So shall your Kingdom come.

NOTES

The opening epigraph is from John Paul II, *"Stay with Us, Lord":*
Mane Nobiscum (Boston: Pauline Books & Media, 2004).

1. Author's translation.
2. "Letters of St. Ignatius of Antioch," in *The Apostolic Fathers,*
trans. Gerald Walsh, SJ (New York: Fathers of the Church, vol. 1,
Christian Heritage Inc., 1947), 120, 111.
3. St. Justin Martyr, *The First Apology,* chaps. 66 and 67, trans.
Thomas B. Falls (New York: Fathers of the Church, vol. 6, Christian
Heritage Inc., 1948), 105.
4. Tertullian, "On Prayer," in *Disciplinary, Moral, and Ascetical
Works,* trans. Sister Emily Joseph Daly, CSJ (New York: Fathers of
the Church Inc, vol. 40, 1959), 164.
5. St. Cyprian, "Treatise 4," in *The Treatises,* trans. Roy J Deferrari
(New York: Fathers of the Church Inc., vol. 36, 1959), 142.
6. St. Eusebius of Caesarea, *Treatise on the Paschal Solemnity,* 7,
9, 10–12: *PG* 24, 701–6. This translation was printed in *A Word In
Season,* vol. 3, Easter, Years I & II (Villanova, PA: Augustinian Press,
2001), 221.
7. St. Cyril of Jerusalem, "Lecture 4," in *The Mystagogical Lectures,*
trans. Anthony A. Stephenson (Washington DC: Fathers of the
Church, vol. 64, Catholic University of America Press, 1970), 181.
8. St. Ambrose, "The Sacraments," in *Theological and Dogmatic
Works,* trans. Roy J. Deferrari (Washington, DC: Fathers of the
Church, vol. 44, Catholic University of America Press, 1963), 304.
9. St. John Chrysostom, "Homilies on the First Letter to the
Corinthians," 24, 4: *PG* 61, 204–5, trans. Anne Field, OSB, in *Christ
Our Light,* vol. 1 (Riverdale, MD: Exordium Books, 1981), 285.
10. St. Augustine of Hippo, "Sermon 272," trans. Anne Field,
OSB, in *Christ Our Light,* vol.1 (Riverdale, MD: Exordium Books,
1981), 279–81.

11. Abbot John Cassian, "The Ninth Conference: On Prayer," in *The Conferences*, trans. Boniface Ramsey, OP (New York: Ancient Christian Writers, The Newman Press, 1997), 343.

12. Saint Peter Chrysologus, "Sermon 67," in *Selected Sermons, PL* 52 (Paris: Migne, 1894), 892; original translation by Ralph Wright, OSB.

13. St. Gregory the Great, "Dialogue 4," Book 4, #59, 60, in *The Dialogues,* trans. Odo Zimmerman, OSB (New York: Fathers of the Church Inc., 1953), 272.

14. John of Damascus, *Exposition of the Orthodox Faith,* Book 4, #13, Nicene and Post–Nicene Fathers, vol. 9, trans. S.D.F. Salmond (New York: The Christian Literature Company, 1899), 83. The parenthetical expression and the italics are in the 1899 translation.

15. St. Bede, "Commentary on St. John's Gospel," 6:37–44, 56–58: *PL* 92 (Paris: Migne 1862), 714, 715, 719; translation by Ralph Wright, OSB.

16. Paschasius Radbertus, *"De Corpore et Sanguine Domini,"* chap. 4, pp. 27–28, lines 3–20, in vol. 16, *Corpus Christianorum Continuatio Mediaevalis* (Belgium: Turnhout 1953). This translation is quoted from *The Hidden Mannah,* James T. O'Connor (San Francisco: Ignatius Press, 2005), 87.

17. St. Odo of Cluny, "The Sacrament of the Body and Blood of the Lord," *PL* 133, (Paris: Migne 1881), 513; original translation by Ralph Wright, OSB.

18. St. Symeon the New Theologian, *The Discourses,* bk. 5, #10, trans. C. J. deCatanzaro (New York: Paulist Press, 1980), 101.

19. *The Prayers and Meditations of St. Anselm,* trans. Benedicta Ward, OSB (Baltimore: Penguin Books Inc., 1973), 100.

20. St. Hildegard, "To an anonymous priest," Epistola 43, *PL*197 (Paris: Migne, 1882), 212–13; original translation by Ralph Wright, OSB.

21. *The Writings of St. Francis of Assisi,* Assisi MS 338, trans. Benen Fahy, OFM (Chicago: Franciscan Herald Press, 1964), 105.

22. St. Bonaventure, *The Tree of Life,* in *Bonaventure,* translated and with an introduction by Ewert Cousins, Classics of Western Spirituality (New York: Paulist Press, 1978), 139.

23. St. Thomas Aquinas, *Opusculum*, 57, 1–4, translation from *The Divine Office*, vol. III. (London: Collins/Dwyer/Talbot, 1974), 31–32.

24. *The Life and Revelations of St. Gertrude the Great,* trans. The Poor Clares of Kenmare (Rockford, IL: TAN Books and Publishers, Inc., 2002), 167.

25. John Tauler. This translation is quoted from *A Word In Season*, vol. 3, Easter Years I & II (Villanova: Augustinian Press, 2001), 256.

26. St. Nicholas Cabasilas. This translation is quoted from *A Word In Season,* vol. 3, Easter Years I & II (Villanova: Augustinian Press, 2001), 204–5.

27. *The Revelations of Divine Love of Julian of Norwich,* trans. James Walsh, SJ (London: Burns & Oates, 1961), 163.

28. St. Catherine of Siena, *The Dialogue,* trans. Suzanne Noffke, OP (New York: Paulist Press, 1980), 210–11.

29. Thomas à Kempis, *The Imitation of Christ,* trans. Ronald Knox and Michael Oakley, IV:2 and IV:3 (New York: Sheed & Ward, 1959), 186 and 189. The author provided an original translation for V:13.

30. St. Thomas More, "A treatice to receave the blessed body of our lorde, sacramentally and virtually bothe," in *The Complete Works of St. Thomas More,* vol.13 (New Haven, CT: Yale University Press, 1976), 191, 192, 200, 201.

31. St. Teresa of Avila, *The Life of Teresa of Jesus,* trans. E. Allison Peers, in *Selected Writings of St. Teresa of Avila,* ed. Wm. J. Doheny, CSC, vol 1, (Milwaukee: Bruce Publishing Company, 1950), 57, 274–75.

32. St. Francis de Sales, *The Love of God: A Treatise,* trans. Vincent Kerns, MSFS (London: Burns & Oates, 1962), 276–77.

33. *The Conferences of St. Vincent de Paul to the Sisters of Charity,* trans. Joseph Leonard, CM, vol. 1 (Maryland: The Newman Press, 1952), 210–12.

34. *Selected Writings of Alphonsus de Liguori: The Practice of the Love of Jesus,* trans. Brendan McConvery, CSsR (New York: Paulist Press, 1999), 119–20.

35. Louise Callan, RSCJ, *Philippine Duchesne: Frontier Missionary of the Sacred Heart, 1769–1852,* (Westminster, MD: The Newman Press, 1965), 96.

36. St. Thérèse of Lisieux, *Story of a Soul,* trans. John Clarke, OCD (Washington, DC: Institute of Carmelite Studies Publications, 1976), 276–77.

37. *Spiritual Autobiography of Charles de Foucauld,* ed. Jean-Francois Six, trans. J. Holland Smith (New York: P. J. Keneday & Sons, 1964), 98–99, 160.

38. Bl. Columba Marmion, *Le Christ Vie de l'Ame [Christ, the Life of the Soul* (originally published in St. Louis, MO: B. Herder Book Company, 1925)]. This translation is quoted from *A Word in Season,* vol. 3, Easter: Year I & II (Villanova, PA: Augustinian Press, 2001), 208.

39. *The Prison Meditations of Father Alfred Delp* (New York: Herder & Herder, 1963), 60, 15, 16.

40. Pope Pius XII, *Mediator Dei (Sacred Liturgy)* 1947, trans. Vatican Web site.

41. Austin Flannery, OP, ed., *Sacrosanctum Concilium: Vatican II Conciliar and Post Conciliar Documents [Constitution on the Sacred Liturgy]* (New York: Costello Publishing Company Inc., 1975).

42. Bl. Teresa of Calcutta, *Jesus, the Word to Be Spoken* (Ann Arbor, MI: Servant Publications, 1998), 74.

43. Archbishop Francis Van Thuan, *Testimony of Hope* (Boston: Pauline Books & Media, 2000), 131.

44. Pope John Paul II, *Ecclesia de Eucharistia (On the Eucharist and Its Relationship to the Church),* 2003, trans. Vatican Web site.

45. Pope Benedict XVI, *Homily at the Mass for World Youth Day 2005,* trans. Vatican Web site.

46. Pope Benedict XVI, *Post-Synodal Apostolic Exhortation Sacramentum Caritatis (Sacrament of Charity), 22 February 2007,* trans. Vatican Web site.

INDEX OF POEMS
WRITTEN OR TRANSLATED
by Ralph Wright, OSB

TITLE/YEAR COMPOSED OR TRANSLATED